The
North Carolina Colony

by Dennis Brindell Fradin

Consultant: Alan D. Watson, Ph.D.
University of North Carolina

 CHILDRENS PRESS ®
CHICAGO

Acknowledgment

For his help, the author thanks Robert J. Cain,
Editor of *Colonial Records of North Carolina*

Library of Congress Cataloging-in-Publication Data

Fradin, Dennis B.
    The North Carolina Colony / by Dennis Brindell Fradin.
        p.   cm. — (The Thirteen Colonies)
    Includes index.
    Summary: Traces the history and people of the colonial period in North
Carolina.
    ISBN 0-516-00396-8
    1. North Carolina—History—Colonial period, ca. 1600-1775—Juvenile
literature. 2. North Carolina—History—Colonial period, ca. 1600-1775—
Biography—Juvenile literature. [1. North Carolina—History—Colonial period,
ca. 1600-1775.] I. Title. II. Series: Fradin, Dennis B. Thirteen Colonies.
F257.F74   1991
975.6'02—dc20   91-13314
                                                                                CIP
                                                                                 AC

Table of Contents

Chapter I

Introducing the Tar Heel State

Down in Carolina grows the lofty pine,
And her groves and forests bear the scented vine;
Here are peaceful homes, too, nestling 'mid the
*   flowers:*
Oh, there is no land on earth like this fair land of
*   ours.*

From "Ho! For Carolina!" by William B.
Harrell

North Carolina is an average-sized state that lies along the Atlantic Ocean in the southeastern United States. It is a southern state. It is an East Coast state. And it was one of the thirteen colonies that England established along the East Coast between 1607 and 1733. The other twelve colonies, in order of their first permanent settlement, were Virginia, Massachusetts, New Hampshire, New York, Connecticut, Maryland, Rhode Island, Delaware, Pennsylvania, New Jersey, South Carolina, and Georgia.

Because of its odd shape, North Carolina is easy to spot in a jigsaw puzzle of the United States.

Opposite page: North Carolina's mountains are known for spectacular fall color. Lighthouses (inset) warn sailors away from North Carolina's dangerous coast.

North Carolina's greatest east-west distance is about 500 miles, making it one of the "fattest" of our 50 states. But its greatest north-south distance is only about 190 miles, making it one of our "shorter" states. Four other southern states are North Carolina's neighbors: Virginia to the north, South Carolina and Georgia to the south, and Tennessee to the west. To the east of North Carolina are the waters of the Atlantic Ocean.

Few states have been the scene of as many momentous events as North Carolina. During the late 1500s Sir Walter Raleigh started England's very first North American colony on North Carolina's Roanoke Island. In one of those settlements, the famous Lost Colony, a baby named Virginia Dare was born in 1587. Little Virginia didn't know it, but she was the first English child born in North America. The fate of Virginia Dare and the rest of the Lost Colony is one of the great mysteries of history.

England's first permanent settlement in America proved to be in Virginia rather than North Carolina. And when present-day North Carolina was first permanently settled in the 1600s, it was by English people who came from Virginia rather than directly from England. For

COLONIAL AMERICA

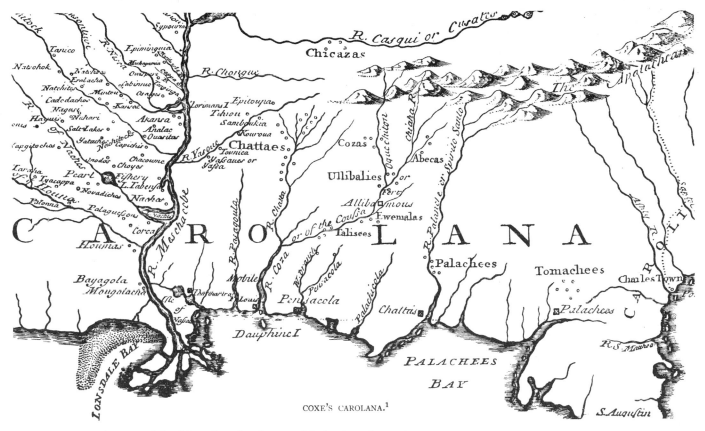

A map of the "Carolana" colony published in the early 1700s

more than 50 years, there was just one colony called *Carolana*—and later *Carolina*. Not until 1712 was the colony formally divided into North Carolina and South Carolina.

North Carolina was one of the poorest—perhaps *the* poorest—of the thirteen colonies. Although some North Carolinians owned slaves, the colony had few rich people. In fact, many outsiders turned up their noses at North Carolina and called it "Rogues' Haven" because it was home to so many debtors, members of religious sects, pirates such as Blackbeard, and other people who wouldn't have been welcome elsewhere.

Poor though they were, the North Carolinians took a back seat to no one in their love of freedom. They became known for their rough and ready ways of defending their rights. An example of this took place in the early 1770s, when western North Carolinians calling themselves "Regulators" rebelled against the colonial government in the east that was mistreating them.

A few years later, when the thirteen colonies broke free of English rule, North Carolina played an important role. North Carolina was the first of the thirteen colonies to declare that it favored independence from England. During the Revolutionary War (1775–1783), about 20,000 North Carolinians helped the nation win its independence. North Carolina was also the site of a major Revolutionary War battle—the Battle of Guilford Courthouse.

Soon after the Revolutionary War ended, American leaders created a set of national laws called the United States Constitution. One by one, the former colonies approved the Constitution, thus becoming states in the new nation. North Carolinians felt that the Constitution took too much power away from the states and the people, and at first rejected it. Thanks partly to demands by North Carolinians, a Bill of Rights was added to the Constitution to protect individuals' and states' rights. North Carolina finally approved the Constitution in 1789, ahead of only Rhode Island of the original thirteen colonies. Also in 1789, North Carolina granted a large tract of land to the federal government that became the state of Tennessee.

For many years, North Carolina remained undeveloped.

Tobacco plant

It had little trade or industry and its roads were poor. As late as 1840, about a third of the state's white people couldn't read or write. Success with tobacco enabled many of its farmers to buy black slaves, so that by 1860 a third of North Carolina's approximately one million people were slaves. The slaves had to work long hours for no pay, and were not educated at all. Many people considered North Carolina so backward in the first half of the 1800s that they called it the Rip Van Winkle State. North Carolina seemed to be sleeping through the years, much like the character Rip Van Winkle in the well-known story.

Things got worse before they got better. By 1860, Southerners were arguing with Northerners over slavery and other matters. In 1860–1861, eleven Southern states including North Carolina left the United States and formed their own country, the Confederate States of America. The Confederate States fought and lost the Civil War against the Union (Northern) states in 1861–1865. Nearly 100 Civil War battles and skirmishes were fought in North Carolina, and about 40,000 of the state's men died of wounds or disease during the war. No other Confederate state lost as many men.

Since the Civil War, North Carolina has awakened from its sleep. One secret of North Carolina's success is that thousands of factories have been built in the state to package its farm goods and natural treasures. Today, North Carolina is not only a top timber-producing state, it also leads the nation in making furniture out of that wood. The state is number one in growing tobacco and manufacturing cigarettes. North Carolina also heads the nation in the manufacture of textiles. Some textiles are made from natural fibers such as cotton, and some are made from nylon and other synthetic fabrics.

Since about the year 1900, North Carolina has also greatly improved its schools and roads. For a while during the 1920s, it was called the Good

Cotton plant

Roads State, but that name didn't catch on. The Old North State—a nickname used in colonial times to distinguish North Carolina from South Carolina—isn't popular anymore either. North Carolina's best-known nickname is the Tar Heel State, and there are several stories about how it originated.

Between 1720 and 1870, North Carolina led the world in producing substances from trees that were used in building and repairing ships. One of these "naval stores" was tar. According to one story, North Carolina tar workers had so much trouble washing the sticky substance off their hands—and even their feet—that people jokingly called them Tar Heels. According to a second story, during the Revolutionary War, British soldiers waded across a river in which North Carolinians had poured tar. The soldiers' feet were so sticky that they had trouble walking when they reached the shore. The mystery of this story is how North Carolinians rather than the British troops became known as Tar Heels. According to a third story, North Carolinians earned the nickname Tar Heels during the Civil War because they stuck to their posts as if tar held them down.

The Tar Heel State has been home to many famous Americans. The nation's eleventh presi-

James Polk

Andrew Johnson

Dolley Madison

dent, James Polk (1795–1849), was born in Pineville, near Charlotte, North Carolina. The seventeenth president, Andrew Johnson (1808–1875), was born in Raleigh, the state capital. We aren't sure which Carolina was the birthplace of Andrew Jackson (1767–1845), the seventh president, but we do know that Jackson studied and practiced law in North Carolina. Dolley Madison (1768–1849), a famous first lady, was born in Guilford County, North Carolina. The wife of President James Madison, Dolley Madison is remembered for saving important items from the White House when the British invaded Washington, D.C., during the War of 1812. And although

12

they were born elsewhere, the inventors Wilbur and Orville Wright performed their greatest feat in North Carolina. On December 17, 1903, the Wright brothers made the world's first airplane flight near Kitty Hawk, North Carolina.

The Wright brothers (inset) made the first flight of a powered aircraft at Kitty Hawk, North Carolina.

A high sand dune at Nags Head, North Carolina

Besides its fascinating history and famous people, North Carolina is an extremely lovely state. Many islands, sand dunes, beaches, and swamps lie along its coast, and several beautiful mountain ranges, including the Blue Ridge, Great Smoky, and Black mountains rise in the west. At 6,684 feet above sea level, Mount Mitchell in the Black

Mountains is the tallest peak in the United States east of the Mississippi River. Forests cover about two-thirds of North Carolina, making it one of the most wooded states. North Carolina also has many attractive rivers, including the Pamlico, the Neuse, the Cape Fear, the Roanoke, the Tar, the Yadkin, and the Catawba.

A bear surveys its domain in the Blue Ridge Mountains.

Chapter II

The Native Americans

*They [the Native Americans] are really better to us
than we are to them. They always give us [food] at
their Quarters, and take care we are armed against
Hunger and Thirst. We do not do so by them . . . but
let them walk by our Doors Hungry and do not often
relieve them. We look upon them with Scorn and
Disdain, and think them little better than Beasts in
Human Shape. . . .*

From Lawson's History of North Carolina
(1709) by John Lawson

Prehistoric people first lived in North Carolina
at least 12,000 years ago. Objects they left behind,
including stone spear points and pottery, reveal a
great deal about the early North Carolinians. At
first they roamed the land, hunting deer and
bears. Such relics as 2,000-year-old corn found
at the Dismal Swamp in northeastern North
Carolina and southeastern Virginia show that
these people learned to farm several thousand
years ago. Farming enabled them to settle down in
villages.

The prehistoric people may have been related to
some of the tribes who lived in North Carolina in

Opposite page:
The Indian village of
Secotan on the Pamlico
River in present-day
North Carolina

17

recent centuries. At least 30,000 (and perhaps many more) Native Americans belonging to about 30 tribes lived in North Carolina before the arrival of Europeans.

The Cherokee were probably the state's largest tribe. They lived in North Carolina's western mountains and also in mountainous regions of South Carolina, Tennessee, Alabama, Georgia, and Virginia. The name *Cherokee* may mean "Mountain People" or "Cave People"—a reference to the Cherokee's love of high places.

The Catawba lived east of the Cherokee in the Catawba (also known as the Wateree) River area of both Carolinas. A number of smaller tribes—including the Waxhaw, the Sugaree, and the Sapona—lived in central North Carolina.

The Tuscarora, who were related to the five Iroquois nations that lived in the New York State region, were the largest tribe of eastern North Carolina. Numbering several thousand people, the Tuscarora inhabited a large area including the site of modern-day Raleigh, North Carolina. Smaller tribes in eastern North Carolina included the Hattera and the Chowan.

Although customs varied from tribe to tribe, North Carolina's Indians had much in common. They lived in villages that usually contained between a few dozen and a few hundred people. Several villages that the Cherokee considered "sacred mother towns" had up to 600 people and were among North Carolina's largest settlements. One of these, the village of Kituwah near present-day Bryson City, may have been the Cherokee's first settlement after they moved from the Great Lakes area to the southeastern United States centuries ago.

The most common type of home among the North Carolina tribes was a hut known as a *wigwam*. It was made by sinking wooden poles into the ground and then covering this framework with bark for the walls and ceiling. Clay was used to plug any holes in the wigwam. The Cherokee wigwams were squarish, but those of other tribes were dome-shaped. Like their cousins up in New York, the Tuscarora lived in longhouses. These were made of the same materials as wigwams, but they were oblong in shape.

Like the Cherokee, the Tuscarora women generally did nearly all of the farming. But in some tribes, such as the Catawba, the men took part in the farm work. The three main crops grown by North Carolina's Indians were corn, beans, and squash, which were widely known among the Native Americans as the "Three

Food was an important part of Native American celebrations.

Sisters." Children picked weeds and scared birds away from the growing crops. Children also helped feed their families by gathering wild raspberries, strawberries, plums, grapes, walnuts, and hickory nuts at various times of the year.

The men provided food for their families by fishing in North Carolina's streams and hunting in its vast forests. They killed such animals as deer, bears, and wild turkeys. Among some tribes, young wasps were considered very tasty. Many Native Americans drank a kind of tea made from a holly plant the Catawba named the *yaupon*.

Animals and plants provided more than just food for the Native Americans. They made clothes, blankets, and moccasins out of animal skins. They turned bird feathers and animal teeth into decorations. Small bones were used as fishing hooks and needles. Babies' diapers were made from moss, while the children's rattles were made from pumpkinlike plants called gourds.

Beaded moccasins

Many people mistakenly think that the Native Americans were a cruel people, perhaps because so many films and books portray them that way. Although they could be cruel to their enemies, the Indians were a loving people in daily life. They rarely hit or yelled at their children. Nothing was too good for their friends and families, and strangers were welcome in their villages. The Tuscarora had a story to explain why people must be kind to strangers. The Creator, they said, sometimes tests people by visiting a home in the body of a stranger. That way the Creator can find out who is truly good-hearted and who is not.

Some tribes had an interesting way to help a family whose home had burned down or who had suffered some other misfortune. The whole village would gather for a feast. During the feast, an old person would explain that bad luck could strike any of them, and that they must help those in need. People would then give food, clothes, and other gifts to the needy family, and help them rebuild their home if it had been lost.

Unlike the Europeans across the Atlantic Ocean, the Native Americans worshiped many gods, rather than just one God. Their main god, the Creator or Great Spirit, was thought to provide good weather, large harvests, and success in war. Almost as powerful was the Evil Spirit, who caused bad weather, poor harvests, and defeat in war. Below these major gods were many lesser gods of the stream, woods, and sky. Religion was important in every aspect of the Indians' lives. Before eating their meal, a family threw a spoonful of food into the fire as an offering to the spirit world. Before wading a stream, an Indian prayed to the water spirit to grant a safe crossing.

The tribes held several yearly religious festivals. Two important Cherokee festivals were the Green Corn Dance and the New Year's Dance. The Green Corn Dance was held in the summer to thank the gods for the year's first corn. The New Year's Dance came in late November, around the time of our modern Thanksgiving. At New Year's, each town put out its sacred fire, which had burned all year. With the lighting of the new sacred fire,

This engraving by John White pictures a Carolina Indian dance.

people were expected to put aside old grudges and make friends with everyone.

In the belief that it brought them closer to the spirit world, the Native Americans often danced and sang for 24 straight hours at their religious festivals. They also smoked tobacco (which the Cherokee called *tsalu*, meaning "fire in the mouth") at their ceremonies because they believed that the smoke carried their prayers up to the gods. However, they did not smoke tobacco in daily life as many people do today.

The Native Americans had no schools. Young people learned to farm, hunt, and fish by working alongside their elders. Stories told by the elders passed on tribal beliefs to the children. We are most familiar with Cherokee stories, partly because many thousands of Cherokee still live in the United States.

One Cherokee story tells of seven boys who, shortly after the creation of the world, spent all their time playing *gatayusti*. This game was played by rolling a disk-shaped stone along the ground and then trying to strike it with spears. The boys wouldn't do anything but play this game, so one day their mothers punished them by setting the *gatayusti* stones in front of them instead of food.

The seven boys were very upset, because it was shameful for Indian children to be punished in any way. The boys decided to leave this world. They formed a circle and danced as they called on the gods to take them up to the Sky World. After a while the boys began to rise. One boy's mother pulled him down with a spear used in the *gatayusti* game, but he came down so hard that he disappeared into the ground. His mother cried over the spot where he had disappeared, and her tears brought him back up out of the ground as the world's first pine tree. The other six boys kept rising until they became the stars the Cherokee called *Anitsutsa* (the Boys)—a group of stars that most people now call the Pleiades.

Scary stories about witches, ghosts, and monsters were also part of Native American lore. The Tuscarora feared the Great Rattlesnake, which was said to have killed many of their people. The Tuscarora also told of a huge white snake that would one day arrive and nearly destroy them as a people.

The Native Americans enjoyed a number of games besides *gatayusti*. One very popular sport, called "the ball game" in English, was played by two opposing teams. Wooden goalposts were set up on opposite sides of a field. Then, using sticks with a leather web on the end, each team tried to send the deerskin ball through the other team's goalposts. Although hands couldn't be used, players were allowed to hit each other with their sticks, which was why this rough game was nicknamed "little brother to war." Sometimes two villages settled a dispute by playing the ball game. The modern sport called lacrosse developed from a form of this game played by tribes in Canada.

Lacrosse developed from a rough game known as "little brother to war."

25

The Native Americans' outlook on life differed from that of the Europeans in many respects. For one thing, the Europeans bought and sold land, while the Native Americans felt that land was like the ocean—something to be enjoyed but not owned. The Native American's sense of justice also differed from the Europeans'. For example, if the Indians couldn't find a murderer, they might kill another member of the murderer's village as a substitute.

The Native Americans were friendly to the first Europeans who came to North Carolina and the other American colonies. In fact, many American colonists would have died without the food and shelter provided by the Indians. Only after many of them were pushed out of their villages, cheated in deals, enslaved, and murdered did some Native Americans fight the colonists. As was true elsewhere, North Carolina's tribes lost these battles to the Europeans, who were more numerous and had better weapons.

North Carolina's Tuscarora people were defeated in what is known as the Tuscarora War (1711–1713). Most of the surviving Tuscarora soon left North Carolina. During the 1830s, long after colonial times, most of the Cherokee in the southeastern United States were forced to move to Oklahoma. So many Cherokee died along the way that they called the trip *Nunna-da-ul-tsun-yi*—"The Place Where They Cried" or "The Trail of Tears." By the mid-1800s only about 1,200 Native Americans remained in North Carolina, some of them Cherokee who had hidden in the Great Smoky Mountains when their people had been forced to move.

Today, the Cherokee have a small reservation in far western North Carolina and about 100,000 Native Americans live in the entire state. Although this is one of the nation's highest Native American populations, it is a small fraction of what the number would be had these peoples been left alone. North Carolina remembers its Native American heritage in many place names, including the following:

Counties	Cities and Towns	Rivers
Alamance	Catawba	Catawba
Alleghany	Cherokee	Chowan
Catawba	Currituck	Pamlico
Cherokee	Indian Trail	Roanoke
Currituck	Roanoke Rapids	Waccamaw
Pamlico	Saxapahaw	
Pasquotank	Wanshese	
Perquimans	Yaupon Beach	

Christopher Columbus arriving in the New World

Chapter III

The Lost Colonies of North Carolina

*We found shallow water, which smelt so sweetly
and was so strong a smell, as if we had been in the
midst of some delicate garden, abounding with all
kinds of odiferous flowers, by which we were
assured that land could not be far distant.*

> *Description by the English sea captain
> Arthur Barlow of his approach to North
> Carolina in 1584*

The Vikings (people from Norway and nearby lands) may have been the first Europeans to explore the Americas. The Vikings are thought to have reached what is now Newfoundland, Canada, around the year A.D. 1000, and they may have also explored parts of the present-day United States at about that time. Although the Vikings built settlements, they did not last. In fact, after a few years the Vikings gave up the idea of colonizing the New World.

As far as we know, about 500 years passed before the next European reached the New World. His name was Christopher Columbus and he was an Italian sailor who was working for Spain. In 1492 Columbus sailed the *Niña*, the *Pinta*, and the *Santa María* across the Atlantic Ocean. Columbus was not looking for the Americas—he did not even know they existed. He was trying to sail west to the lands known as the Indies (India, China, Japan, and other Asian lands) where Europeans wanted to obtain gold, spices, and other treasures. On October 12, 1492, Columbus reached the Bahama Islands off the coast of Florida. Thinking that he had reached the Indies, he called the people he met "Indians," and the

An early map of the New World made after the discoveries of Columbus and Balboa

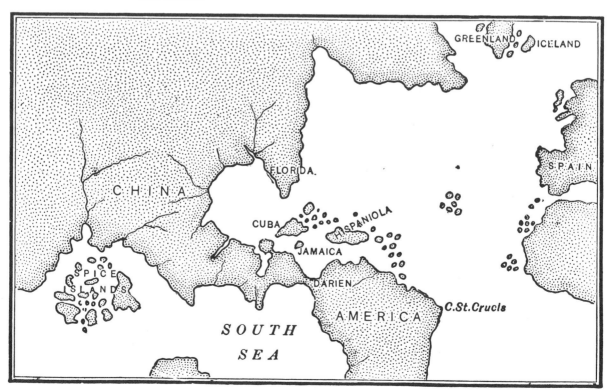

name stuck. In all, Columbus made four trips to the Americas between 1492 and 1504. Although he never reached what is now the United States, Columbus did visit parts of South and Central America.

To his dying day, Columbus seems to have thought that he had reached Asia. The Italian explorer Amerigo Vespucci was the first European to realize that the landmass Columbus had visited was a previously unknown continent. While on a voyage to South America for Portugal in 1501–1502, Vespucci realized that the landmass went too far south to be Asia. Because Amerigo Vespucci discovered their true nature, the Americas were given his first name, with a slight change in spelling.

Amerigo Vespucci

Meanwhile, the voyages of Columbus had paved the way for Spain to colonize much of Central and South America. The Spanish grew rich from their American colonies. They obtained gold and silver in the New World and also built many large farms called plantations. The tragedy was that they enslaved and killed many thousands of native peoples in the process.

Other European nations envied Spain's success in the New World. They, too, wanted to obtain riches and build farms in the Americas. This part

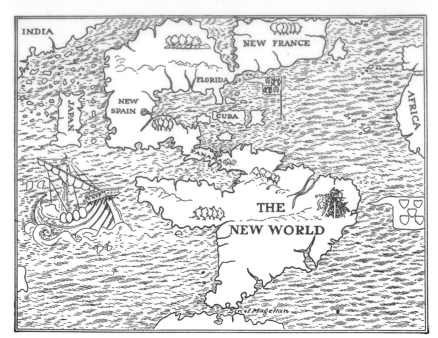

The New World according to a map-maker of 1540

of the world had yet another attraction. Many people believed that a river cut across all of North America from east to west. Such a waterway would be a shortcut to Asia. Several explorers came to North America in the late 1400s and the 1500s searching for this shortcut.

In 1497 John Cabot, who was working for England, sailed to America to search for the shortcut to Asia. Cabot reached either Newfoundland or Nova Scotia in Canada, but did not find the legendary passage to Asia. (No such natural waterway exists except in far northern Canada.) Cabot's voyage was very important, though, because it was the basis for England's claim to North America.

A few years later, France also became involved in North American exploration, and this was when the region that is now North Carolina entered the picture. In early 1524 Giovanni da Verrazano, an Italian working for France, sailed the *Dauphine* to America in search of the fabled Asian shortcut. The first land Verrazano reached was Cape Fear in North Carolina, where he arrived in March 1524. Then, as now, North Carolina was lovely in the spring, and Verrazano wrote a glowing report of the region. He then sailed north all the way to the Canadian coast just beyond Maine. Along the way, Verrazano added several other "firsts" to his list. Besides having become the first known European to reach North Carolina, Verrazano became the first known European to explore New York and Rhode Island.

Giovanni da Verrazano

SPAIN ATTEMPTS A COLONY

Spain, rather than England or France, continued to be the main power in the Americas for the rest of the 1500s. Although Spain never achieved the hold on the present-day United States that it had on Central and South America, the country did begin to colonize what is now the southeastern United States during the 1500s. In 1526 Spaniards may have made a major attempt to settle present-day North Carolina and South Carolina. That summer the Spanish official Lucas Vásquez de Ayllón led about 500 people from the Spanish-held city of Santo Domingo (in what is now the island country of the Dominican Republic) north to the mainland. Most of these people were Spanish men and women, but among them were a few slaves, probably the first African slaves brought into what is now the United States.

The Spaniards built a settlement that may have been located at the place where North Carolina's Cape Fear River empties into the Atlantic Ocean. It didn't last long. Because of starvation and disease, Ayllón soon moved the colony south, but that didn't help. By the fall of 1526, more than two-thirds of the colonists, including Ayllón, were dead. In October the remaining 150 colonists gave up and returned to Santo Domingo.

The Spaniards had more success in Florida. In the fall of 1565 they founded St. Augustine, Florida, now the oldest European-built city in the United States. Spain held the Florida region almost continuously until 1821, when the United States finally took control of the area.

ENGLAND ENTERS THE PICTURE
After the Spanish founded St. Augustine, people

Ships like these were used to explore new countries.

in England realized that if they didn't act soon Spain might seize land north of Florida. Under Queen Elizabeth I, who ruled from 1558 to 1603, England grew into a great world power. Some English people, including the soldier and explorer Walter Raleigh, became very interested in colonizing America. In the spring of 1584, Queen Elizabeth issued a charter allowing Raleigh to build an American colony at an unnamed spot.

First, Raleigh sent a small expedition to find a good site for his colony. His two ships departed for America under the command of Philip Amadas and Arthur Barlow in April 1584. An English artist named John White was one of the men who sailed with them.

After a voyage of about two months, the ships approached North Carolina on July 4, 1584. About that time, Barlow wrote the words that begin this chapter, telling how wonderful North Carolina smelled. The two ships spent a few weeks exploring the Outer Banks—the islands, reefs, sand dunes, and sandbars that form a kind of barrier off mainland North Carolina. Somewhere along the North Carolina coast during that summer of 1584, Amadas and Barlow held a ceremony in which they claimed the present-day United States for England. In the area of Roanoke Island they met friendly Indians, and asked one of them his name for North Carolina. Not understanding English, the Indian answered *Wingandacon*, meaning "You wear good clothes" in his language. As a result, for a few months the English called the colony Wingandacon!

After spending nearly two months along North Carolina's coast, Amadas and Barlow departed around mid-August. Besides their plant and animal samples and written reports, they brought home two Native Americans named Manteo and Wanchese who apparently went along willingly. By

An illustration by John White for Sir Walter Raleigh's book, *Voyage into Virginia*

mid-September 1584, the expedition was back in England.

The arrival of the explorers and Indians and the prospect of settling America stirred great excitement in England. Over the next few months, Raleigh organized an expedition to begin settling the new colony. Then on January 6, 1585, Queen Elizabeth performed two historic acts. For helping to begin English colonization of America, the queen knighted Raleigh, meaning that from then on he was *Sir* Walter Raleigh. That same day the queen changed the name of the American land from Wingandacon to Virginia, probably at Sir Walter's suggestion.

Sir Walter Raleigh

The name *Virginia* had a double meaning. First, it honored Elizabeth, who was called the "Virgin Queen" because she never married.

But the word *virgin* can also mean "fresh or unspoiled," and the new land seemed very fresh and unspoiled compared to England, which in places had become dirty and crowded.

Virginia at that time included not only present-day Virginia but also the Carolinas and several other states. Only later was this huge area divided into separate colonies. Raleigh planned to establish his colony on Roanoke Island, off the coast of

Queen Elizabeth I

what is now North Carolina.

By the spring of 1585, Raleigh had organized a seven-ship fleet and about 600 men to start England's first American colony, which was intended as a military outpost. Among the leaders were Ralph Lane (who would govern the colony), Sir Richard Grenville, and Philip Amadas. Several hundred of the men were soldiers, for Raleigh knew that this "Ralph Lane colony" might have to defend itself against the Spaniards and perhaps the Indians. Also among the passengers were the artist John White, the astronomer and mathematician Thomas Hariot, and Manteo and Wanchese who were returning home.

Sir Richard Grenville

The fleet reached North Carolina's Outer Banks in late June 1585. Before going to Roanoke Island, the Englishmen visited several villages along the coast. According to their custom, the tribes welcomed the newcomers. On these visits, John White drew some of the pictures that provide us with so much of what we know about the Native Americans. At one town, however, the Englishmen found that a silver cup of theirs was missing. Assuming that the Indians had stolen it, Grenville took revenge by burning the entire village and its cornfields. This cruel and stupid act turned the

Raleigh's expedition at Roanoke Island (map) traded with the Native Americans.

Native Americans against the Englishmen—and helped doom the colony.

The expedition finally reached Roanoke Island in late July 1585. The carpenters and construction workers Raleigh had sent began building Fort Raleigh, as well as some cottages, on the island. But Grenville soon departed for England with most of the men to obtain more supplies for the colony, and only about 100 men were left on

Roanoke to maintain the "city of Raleigh," the first English settlement in America. (It had nothing to do with the city of Raleigh, North Carolina, which was founded two centuries later and more than 150 miles to the west.)

Almost everything went wrong with the Ralph Lane colony. The leaders argued and the men ran short of food. After seeing what Englishmen would do over the loss of a drinking cup, many Native Americans gave up the idea of helping them. Wingina, the chief of the small Roanoke tribe in the area, decided to destroy the colony with the help of other tribes. But Lane learned of Wingina's plan and attacked and killed the Roanoke chief in late spring of 1586, ending this threat.

A few days after the murder of Wingina, word reached the Roanoke colonists that the famous sea captain Sir Francis Drake was coming with a fleet of more than 20 ships. Drake had become the first English person to sail around the world a few years earlier, and had recently raided Spanish possessions in Florida and along the Caribbean Sea. Before returning to England, Drake was stopping at Roanoke Island to see how Sir Walter Raleigh's colonists were doing.

Governor Ralph Lane met Drake on his ship, where Sir Francis made a generous offer. If they wanted, the Roanoke colonists could all return with Drake to England immediately. If the colonists didn't want to do that, Drake would leave a ship and a month's supplies. The colonists could then return to England at the end of the month if they chose. Lane accepted the second offer. He figured that the colonists could hold out at least a month longer while awaiting the supplies that Sir Richard Grenville was expected to send.

Sir Francis Drake and his famous ship the *Golden Hind*

Mother Nature wrecked this plan, however. On June 13, 1586, a fierce storm slammed into the North Carolina coast, scattering and damaging

Sir Francis Drake's fleet. The ship that Drake had offered to leave with Lane was blown out to sea, and the only ship that Drake could now spare wasn't as good.

Lane and the colony's other leaders then decided to abandon the colony and go back to England with Sir Francis Drake. They sailed with Drake on June 19, 1586, abandoning three colonists who were away from the settlement at the time. It also appears that several hundred African and Indian slaves who had been captured by Drake during his raids on Spanish possessions were also abandoned on Roanoke Island.

THE FIRST TWO LOST COLONIES

The Ralph Lane colony that had lasted about a year on Roanoke Island was England's first American colony. If that fierce storm had not struck in June 1586, it might have been England's first permanent colony. That storm had forced Lane and all but three of his men to sail with Sir Francis Drake, instead of staying in North Carolina another month. As it turned out, the events that unfolded over that month might have breathed new life into the Ralph Lane colony. A short time after the colony was abandoned (perhaps just a day later) a supply ship sent by Sir Walter Raleigh reached Roanoke Island. And a few weeks after that, Grenville arrived with eight ships and a year's supplies.

What became of the three Englishmen left behind by Lane, and the African and Indian slaves that Drake was thought to have abandoned on Roanoke Island? The only signs ever found by Grenville and his men were the remains of two people—an Englishman and an Indian—who had been hanged. Why they had been killed, and what happened to the other two Englishmen and the abandoned slaves is a mystery. They were the first lost colony of North Carolina, though not the most famous. Before returning to England in late 1586, Grenville left between 15 and 18 men on Roanoke Island to try to re-establish the colony.

Despite its failure, the Ralph Lane colony had inspired great interest in American settlement. If English people could survive in America for a year, couldn't a permanent colony be built? Dozens of pictures John White had drawn of the region, plus a book by Thomas Hariot called *Brief and True Report of the New Found Land of Virginia*, also stirred up interest in the New World. Sir Walter Raleigh recruited more people to

The landing of Raleigh's "Lost Colony" settlers at Roanoke Island

attempt another settlement in Virginia. This time he signed up families instead of just men, because families were more likely to put down roots.

Sir Walter Raleigh named the artist John White to govern his new colony. Among the more than 100 people who made the move to America were White's daughter, Eleanor, and her husband, Ananias Dare.

The expedition left England on May 8, 1587. Raleigh had chosen another location for this colony. After stopping at Roanoke Island to pick up the 15 to 18 men left there by Grenville, White was to sail farther north and build his colony along Chesapeake Bay (in the region of modern-day Virginia, Maryland, and Delaware). Raleigh and the others who planned this expedition wanted a different location because they felt that the North Carolina coast was too hazardous for ships and that the Indians on Roanoke Island were too angry for another colony to be attempted.

When the White colonists reached Roanoke Island in late July 1587, a human skeleton was all they found of the 15 to 18 men who had been left there the previous year. Friendly Indians told the colonists that the men had been invited by Indians to a supposedly peaceful talk, but once there, the men had been attacked. At least one colonist had been killed, but some of the others had escaped in a boat and had disappeared without a trace. No one knows what became of the other men left by Grenville—they were North Carolina's second lost colony.

THE FAMOUS LOST COLONY

Governor John White planned to continue north to Chesapeake Bay to establish the new colony, as Sir Walter Raleigh had directed. However, the commander of the expedition's ships refused to sail the ships there—perhaps he was afraid to enter a region he hadn't visited before. In any event, White and his colonists had to remain on Roanoke Island.

The colonists set to work repairing the fort and the old cottages and building new cottages. Just several days after their arrival, an Englishman named George Howe wandered two miles from the fort while gathering crabs. No doubt remembering how Lane and his men had killed their chief, Wingina, Roanoke Indians shot Howe full of arrows and then smashed his skull.

A few days after George Howe's death, the little colony was the scene of two happy events. On August 13, 1587, the colonists' friend Manteo of the small Croatoan tribe adopted the Christian faith. His was the first known Protestant baptism in what is now the United States. Five days later, on August 18, 1587, Eleanor White Dare gave birth to a baby girl. Governor John White explained in his journal why his new granddaughter was named Virginia Dare:

> *Eleanor, daughter of the Governor, and wife to Ananias Dare . . . was delivered of a daughter in Roanoke . . . and because this child was the first Christian born in Virginia, she was named Virginia.*

Governor White and his people soon faced serious problems. They had arrived too late in the year to plant corn and other crops, so they needed

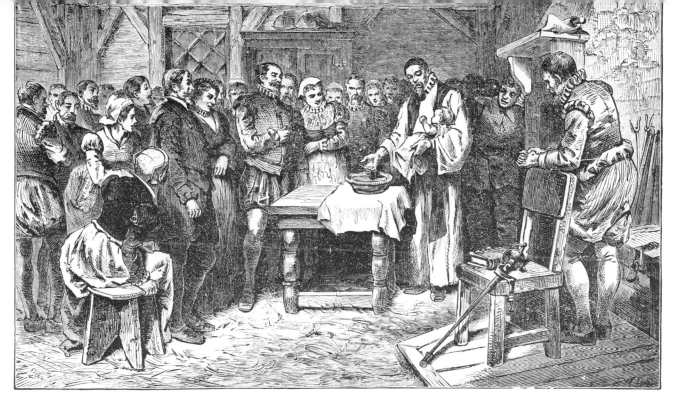
The baptism of Virginia Dare

food as well as more supplies. Even tribes who had been friendly, such as the Croatoan, now had good reason to stay away from the English people instead of helping them. Despite his peaceful nature, Governor White had decided to punish the Roanoke Indians for killing George Howe, but his men had mistakenly attacked a group of Croatoans instead!

By late August 1587 the ships that had brought the colony to Roanoke Island were ready to return to England. It was also clear by then that one of the colonists had to return to England for food and supplies. Governor White wanted to stay and

47

run his colony, but he couldn't convince anyone else to go. Just nine days after his grand-daughter's birth, Governor White said good-bye to his family and friends and sailed for England. Before leaving, however, he gave them some instructions. If the colonists had to leave the "city of Raleigh" while he was gone, they were to carve the name of their destination on a tree near the fort. If they left in danger, they were to carve a cross above the destination.

Governor White got bad news when he reached England in November 1587. Sir Walter Raleigh wanted to help his American colony, but couldn't. England was about to be attacked by a huge fleet called the Spanish Armada, and needed its best ships. In April 1588, White was allowed to sail for America with two ships that were too small to fight the Armada, but he had to return to England after a fight with two French vessels. Sir Francis Drake and other great English sea captains defeated the Spanish Armada in the summer of 1588, but—for reasons that aren't quite clear—White had to wait until early spring of 1590 before returning to America.

We can imagine John White's excitement as his expedition approached Roanoke Island that summer of 1590. White finally reached the fort in

August, around the time of Virginia Dare's third birthday, but there were no people in the "city of Raleigh" to greet him. As the disappointed governor looked around he found two clues. Carved on one tree was part of a word—CRO. Carved on another tree was the whole word—CROATOAN. And no cross had been carved above either word. Evidently the colonists had gone to live with friendly Croatoan Indians on the island that the colonists called Croatoan (now Hatteras Island).

The only clue to the Lost Colony's fate was the word *Croatoan* carved on a tree.

John White was very eager to visit Croatoan Island, which was just a short way from Roanoke Island. But after waiting three years and sailing thousands of miles across the Atlantic Ocean, he was prevented from traveling those last few miles to search for his family and friends. Stormy weather, a mishap in which seven men drowned, and a shortage of food and fresh water forced the expedition to give up and sail back to England. John White died without ever knowing what had become of his loved ones and the third lost colony of North Carolina—the famous Lost Colony. Four centuries have passed and we still don't know what became of Virginia Dare and the other colonists.

There have been a few hints at what may have happened. In 1607, Jamestown, Virginia (about 120 miles north of Roanoke Island), became the first permanent English settlement in America. The Jamestown colonists heard from the Indians about people in the Virginia-North Carolina region who dressed, looked, and lived like English people. According to other reports, Chief Powhatan of Virginia's Powhatan Indians admitted having killed many of the people of the Lost Colony.

Several theories have been presented. Some people think the colonists may have lived and intermarried with the Indians, and that some people of Indian heritage who live in southeastern North Carolina today are descendants of the Lost Colony. If that is true, the descendants of Virginia Dare may be living in North Carolina right now. Another theory is that most of the Roanoke colonists went to present-day Virginia where many of them were killed by Powhatan's order. Even if that happened, a few people may have survived and could have descendants living today. A third theory is that the colonists tried to reach England in a boat Governor White left with them, but were lost at sea.

The importance of the three lost colonies was that they were the first steps in the permanent English colonization of America. The English learned from the mistakes they had made with these first efforts, and this helped them succeed later. Among the North Carolina place names that remind us of the lost colonies are Dare County (named for Virginia Dare); Raleigh, the state capital (named for Sir Walter Raleigh); and the town of Manteo in Dare County (named for the colonists' Indian friend).

SIR WALTER RALEIGH (1552?–1618)

Sir Walter Raleigh

Walter Raleigh was born into a prominent family in southwestern England in either 1552 or 1554. He never spelled his last name "Raleigh" as far as we know. Until he was about 30 he usually wrote "Rauley," but then he switched to "Ralegh." Today, most people spell it Raleigh—like the North Carolina capital that was later named for him.

As a boy, Walter was well educated, perhaps by a tutor in his home. He entered Oxford University at about the age of 16, but did not stay long. Instead he went off to France at about 17 to fight for a persecuted Protestant group known as the Huguenots. Raleigh made a name for himself as a soldier, fighting in such places as Ireland and Spain and suffering several wounds. In recognition of his services, Queen Elizabeth granted him a large tract of land in Ireland. It was on this land that Raleigh planted the first potatoes in Ireland—one of his most famous achievements.

Although he could be brutal in war, Sir Walter had a gentle side. He wrote beautiful poems, including some to Queen Elizabeth, who grew fond of him. According to a famous story, the queen was out walking one wet day when she came to a muddy spot. She was about to walk around it when Raleigh, who wore very costly clothes, spread his cloak upon the mud for her to walk across. Queen Elizabeth supported Raleigh's efforts to colonize America during the 1580s. She knighted him in 1585, and two years later she made him Captain of the Queen's Guard, which meant that he was responsible for her safety.

In 1591, Sir Walter secretly married Elizabeth Throckmorton, one of the queen's servants. When Queen Elizabeth learned about this in 1592, she was enraged. As part of the queen's inner circle, Raleigh was supposed to tell her about important events in his life. The queen may have also been jealous of this other Elizabeth. As punishment, Queen Elizabeth locked the couple in the prison known as the Tower of London for several months.

Raleigh had lost a fortune while trying to colonize North Carolina, and after his marriage he also lost the queen's friendship. He began planning an expedition that he hoped would please the queen and earn a fortune for himself. It was said that along South America's northern coast was a place called El Dorado, a land of great riches where the hills were made of gold and the rivers were filled with pearls. Since Spain also claimed parts of South America's northern coast, Raleigh figured that he could attack the Spanish while discovering El Dorado. Raleigh led an expedition into the region of present-day Venezuela in 1595, but found no treasure and won no great triumphs over the Spanish. Queen Elizabeth died in 1603 without ever forgiving him.

Title page of Raleigh's book

England's next monarch, King James I, was afraid that Raleigh might want to kill him and place someone else on the throne. The king had Raleigh charged with treason (serious crimes against the government). Although Raleigh seems to have been innocent of the charges, he was found guilty and sent to the Tower of London again. This time he spent twelve years in the Tower. While there he wrote his *History of the World*, which was a very popular book during the 1600s.

Raleigh figured that the king would free him if there was something to be gained by it. Sir Walter sent messages to the king promising to bring back a treasure of gold from South America if he were released. The king finally freed Raleigh in 1616 and allowed him to return to South America the next year. However, this time Raleigh was forbidden to attack the Spanish. This expedition was a total disaster. Raleigh found no gold mines, and, while he was ill and unable to lead them, his men attacked a Spanish town.

Upon his return to England in 1618, Raleigh was once more locked in the Tower of London. The king was angry at him for allowing the attack on the Spanish and for not bringing back gold. Raleigh was sentenced to die. People who witnessed the execution were amazed by Raleigh's courage. On the way to his execution, Raleigh spotted a bald-headed man. Sir Walter took off his cap and gave it to the man, joking that "Thou hast more need of it now than I." A few minutes later the man who had begun the colonization of America was beheaded.

JOHN WHITE (1540?–?)

John White was probably born in England, but we don't know where or when. Judging by his later work, he must have been trained as an artist, but nothing is known about that either. We do know that in the late 1500s White made several trips to America as an artist and later as a governor.

Whenever explorers visit new places, the people back home are curious. For example, when men first walked on the moon on July 20, 1969, half a billion earthlings watched the TV pictures that the astronauts sent home. When Christopher Columbus and others began exploring the Americas in the late 1400s and the 1500s, the people back home were curious, too. There were no cameras yet, so the explorers began taking artists along to draw pictures and make maps of the New World's wonders.

Between 1576 and 1578, the English navigator Sir Martin Frobisher

Drawings of Native Americans by John White show fishing methods (above), a warrior (right), and a medicine man (far right).

made three trips to Canada. John White apparently went with Frobisher as his artist at least once, because we have several pictures that White made of Eskimos and how they lived. White's ability must have impressed Sir Walter Raleigh, who hired him as artist for the expedition that started England's first American colony on Roanoke Island in 1585–1586. Although this colony failed, John White painted a wonderful group of watercolors based on what he saw on that expedition. White's paintings bring the Indians, plants, and animals of the region to life—much more so than the writings of the time which seem so old-fashioned to us.

In early 1587 Sir Walter Raleigh chose John White to govern the new colony he planned to establish in America that year. This was as poor a decision on Raleigh's part as marrying the queen's maid and then not telling the queen. Although John White was an excellent artist, he was too gentle a soul to make a good governor. He allowed the commander of the expedition's ships to bully him into settling the colony on Roanoke Island again, instead of farther north on Chesapeake Bay where Raleigh wanted. Then a few weeks later Governor White made his greatest blunder. He let the colonists talk him into returning to England for supplies, when he should have ordered someone else to go rather than leave the colony without a governor. But White disliked giving orders, and when no one else wanted to go, he agreed to make the voyage himself.

When he said good-bye to his daughter, his son-in-law, and his newborn granddaughter Virginia Dare, White must have known that he might never see them again. Ocean voyages were very dangerous back then, and he probably thought that he might die at sea. This nearly happened in 1588 during White's failed attempt to reach Roanoke Island. His ship got into a fight with two French vessels, resulting in the deaths of several of his fellow passengers. White survived being cut on the head with a sword, struck on the head with a weapon called a pike, and shot in the rear end with a gun. His ship had to return to England. When White finally reached Roanoke Island two years later, his loved ones and the rest of the colonists had disappeared.

We aren't sure what became of John White after this, although we know that in 1593 he was living in Ireland. Some people believe he died that year, but he may have lived to make one more attempt to reach his family in the early 1600s. His artwork remains one of our main sources for knowing what North America was like before the Europeans came.

MAGNUM · SIGILLUM · CAROLINÆ · DOMINORUM

DOMITUS ORBIS
CULTORIBUS

A Carolina settler's
home. Inset: The seal
of the Lords Proprietors.

Chapter IV

When Carolina Was Young: 1620s–1705

North Carolina is a vale of humility between two mountains of conceit [Virginia and South Carolina].

Old North Carolina saying

The Spanish Armada, bad weather, bad luck, and the colonists' cruelty toward the Indians had prevented North Carolina from being the site of England's first permanent American colony. This honor went to Jamestown, Virginia, which was settled by about 100 English colonists in the spring of 1607.

English people came to what is now Virginia for several reasons. Some colonists wanted land. According to the laws in England at the time, the oldest son inherited most of his father's land and possessions, leaving many younger sons rather poor. (Females were largely excluded from the inheritance picture back then.) Some of these younger sons came to Virginia because they could own land there. Other people came in search of gold and silver or to seek adventure. The settlement of Virginia proved to be very important to North Carolina, but not for a few years.

At first, Virginia was under the control of a private firm called the Virginia Company, which claimed that the colony covered a large part of what is now the United States. In 1624, England's King James I (for whom Jamestown had been named) seized control of Virginia from the Virginia Company and turned it into a royal colony—one directly ruled by England's kings and queens. This meant that the monarchs could divide the huge region called Virginia any way they chose.

King Charles I

King James I died in 1625 and his son, Charles I, became king that same year. In 1629 King Charles I lopped off a huge area south of modern-day Virginia and gave it to Sir Robert Heath, an important English official. This territory included all of North Carolina except about 50 miles in the north, all of South Carolina, and all of Georgia except about 50 miles in the south. King Charles I named this territory *Carolana* (meaning "Land of Charles" in Latin).

Sir Robert Heath worked out a plan to settle French Huguenots in Carolana. The Huguenots were Protestants who had been persecuted by the

The settlers traded with the Native Americans.

Roman Catholic leaders in France, and many of them were seeking a new home. This plan did not work out, though. The only English people in Carolana during the 1630s and 1640s were a few visitors from Virginia who went there to explore or perhaps to trade with the Indians.

By the mid-1600s, it was becoming difficult to obtain good land in the settled parts of Virginia, and some Virginians began moving into what is now North Carolina. A Virginian named Nathaniel Batts may have been the first permanent colonist

Edward Hyde

George Monck

Anthony Ashley Cooper

in Carolana. By 1655, Batts had built a house on Albemarle Sound in what is now northeastern North Carolina. More Virginians entered Carolana's northern areas during the late 1650s. By 1660 about 1,000 people lived in Carolana, all of them in what is now North Carolina. Present-day South Carolina wasn't permanently settled until 1670.

Charles I, the king for whom Carolana had been named, was beheaded in 1649. For eleven years thereafter, England had no king or queen, but was ruled by powerful lawmakers. During those years, some people who were loyal to the family of the dead Charles I worked to make his son, Charles II, the king of England. Finally, in 1660, Charles II did become king. After taking the throne, Charles II rewarded many of the people who had remained loyal to his family.

In the spring of 1663, Charles II granted Carolana to eight such loyal noblemen. The eight were Edward Hyde, Earl of Clarendon; George Monck, Duke of Albemarle; Anthony Ashley Cooper; William, Earl of Craven; Sir George Carteret; Sir John Colleton; and two brothers, Sir William Berkeley and John, Lord Berkeley. Carolana was now a proprietary, or privately owned, colony, and the eight landlords were called the Lords Proprietors. Also in 1663, the spelling of *Carolana* was changed to *Carolina*, as we write it today. Nearly half a century would pass before Carolina was divided into North Carolina and South Carolina, however.

In 1665, King Charles II enlarged Carolina so that it extended north up to about the northern boundary of present-day North Carolina and south into Florida. At that time, Carolina stretched west all the way to the Pacific Ocean. If the Carolinas hadn't later given up the territory south and west of their present borders, the United States map would be much different today. The cities of Nashville (Tennessee), Tulsa (Oklahoma), Amarillo (Texas), Santa Fe (New Mexico), Flagstaff (Arizona), and Bakersfield (California) would all be in North Carolina!

The Lords Proprietors announced in 1665 that they were creating three governmental units called counties in Carolina. The southernmost county, Craven, was located along the Ashley and Cooper rivers in what is now South Carolina. The settlement of this region in 1670 by English people marked the first permanent colonization of present-day South Carolina.

The middle county, Clarendon, was in present-day southeastern North Carolina along the Cape

William, Earl of Craven

Signatures of the Lords Proprietors

Fear River. For part of the 1660s several hundred English people from such places as Massachusetts and the British-ruled island of Barbados settled in this area. However, by 1667 these English people had abandoned their settlements because of supply shortages, disputes with the Native Americans, and other reasons that are unclear today. In 1667, Clarendon County passed out of existence.

The northernmost of the three counties—Albemarle—proved to be the seed of North Carolina. Located in the Albemarle Sound area in what is now northeastern North Carolina, Albemarle County was the region that Virginians had settled in the 1650s and early 1660s. Virginians continued to move into this area during the late 1600s. By 1680, present-day North Carolina had about 5,500 colonists, all of them living in the Albemarle Sound region. By 1690, the colonial population had grown to about 8,000, but North Carolina had no towns as yet and the colonists lived on farms scattered across the countryside.

North Carolina in those days was almost like one big forest, so the settlers had plenty of wood for building materials. The first English colonists usually built log homes. Since glass was difficult to obtain in early colonial times, generally the windows in the homes were only openings in the walls covered by wooden shutters. The early colonists also made their own chairs, tables, and bed frames out of wood.

The colonists' main crop was corn. Many families began the day by eating a puffed-kernel corn dish called hominy. During the course of the day they also ate corn bread, corn stews, and corn on the cob. Corn whiskey was a popular drink among adults. Many people slept on mattresses stuffed with corn husks. And those parts of the corn plant that the people didn't use were fed to the farm animals.

A frontier farmer

Corn wasn't the colonists' only food, though. They also grew beans, peas, potatoes, rice, sweet potatoes, and wheat. They got milk from their cows, bacon from their hogs, and eggs from their chickens. Nearly every man hunted and fished in colonial times. They brought home venison (deer meat), wild turkeys and ducks, trout, catfish, bass, and many other kinds of animals and fish for the family table.

Families bartered (traded) with each other a great deal. There were no refrigerators in those days and meat soon spoiled, so a family that had killed a deer might trade some venison to another family for milk and cheese. A man who came home with a string of fish might trade half of them for a basket of eggs.

The North Carolinians also produced a crop that wasn't eaten—tobacco. Ever since the Virginian John Rolfe had shipped some tobacco leaves to England in 1613, there had been a demand for the American-grown crop. King Charles I supposedly once said that Virginia was "founded upon smoke," meaning that tobacco had made it successful. North Carolina had the proper soil and climate for growing tobacco, but it had a major drawback compared to Virginia.

The only way to send the tobacco to the main market—England—was by ship. Many of Virginia's large tobacco plantations were built right on deep-water harbors. Big ships came right up to the warehouses and loaded the tobacco barrels. However, because of the sandbars and reefs of the Outer Banks, large ships had trouble reaching the North Carolina shore. This accident of geography hampered North Carolinians from trading their tobacco and other products, and was a big reason for the colony's poverty. Some colonial North Carolinians took their tobacco over poor roads to Virginia ports, where it was shipped to England. And some smaller ships docked along

Poor roads made transport of the tobacco crop to market a difficult task.

the North Carolina shore, where they picked up tobacco and carried it to such countries as Scotland, The Netherlands, and France. However, it wasn't until the 1800s that tobacco started to become the tremendous money crop for North Carolina that it is today.

In Virginia, the rich planters bought large numbers of African slaves to work on their tobacco plantations. Some wealthy Virginians built gigantic plantations that were worked by hundreds of slaves. But in North Carolina, which had few wealthy people compared to Virginia, slavery didn't play a major role until about the mid-1700s. In 1690, for example, only about 300 of North Carolina's 8,000 non-Indians were slaves, while about 10,000 of Virginia's 55,000 non-Indians were slaves.

By the 1690s, North Carolina was one of the poorest regions in the American colonies. Most families who could afford it preferred to live in Virginia and other colonies that had better roads and deep-water ports. Besides attracting poorer colonial families, North Carolina was also a refuge for runaway servants and slaves. In addition, North Carolina allowed religious groups to live there that would have been persecuted elsewhere.

An English group that called themselves the Religious Society of Friends began arriving in what is now North Carolina around 1672. Other people mockingly called them "Quakers" because George Fox, who founded the group around 1647, had once said that people should "tremble at the word of the Lord." Today the Friends are still called Quakers, but not in the insulting way that the term was used back in the 1600s.

The Quakers dressed and lived simply because they felt that spiritual values were more important than riches. Several of their other

Above: George Fox.
Left: A Quaker trial.

beliefs made them unpopular in England. For one
thing, since they felt that all people have a bit of
God in them, they treated the poorest beggar the
same as the richest nobleman. Since they opposed
war, they refused to serve in England's army. And
instead of having ministers, they let anyone who
felt inspired by God speak at their meetings.
Between 1661 and the early 1680s, about 15,000
of these peace-loving people were jailed in
England. To escape persecution, thousands of
Quakers sought religious freedom in America.

William Penn pledges friendship with the Native Americans.

The main Quaker haven in America was Pennsylvania, which the great Quaker William Penn founded in 1681. Quakers also moved to other colonies. A number of them came to North Carolina after being mistreated in Virginia. George Fox, the founder of the religion, visited North Carolina's Albemarle region during the 1670s. The Quakers made so many converts there that by about the year 1700 they made up about one-seventh of North Carolina's colonial population.

A religious group called the Baptists began moving into North Carolina in the 1690s. A few years later, several other religious groups joined the Quakers and the Baptists in North Carolina. Today the United States boasts of being a "melting pot" because of its human variety, but in colonial times many people frowned on North Carolina because of its religious openness. The colony was even called "Rogues' Haven," partly because it attracted so many people who didn't belong to the Church of England.

The North Carolinians were a very independent bunch. In 1665, the Lords Proprietors provided them with a set of laws called the Concessions and Agreement. According to this document, the Lords Proprietors were allowed to appoint a governor for Albemarle County, which was what North Carolina was called at this point. William Drummond, the first governor, served from 1664 to 1667. The governor was allowed to appoint helpers called a Council. But the people also had certain rights. The voters (who were all male) were allowed to elect a legislature called the Assembly which could pass and repeal laws. Also, the people of Albermarle County didn't have to pay any taxes except a rent on their land called a quitrent. The quitrent was to be given to the Lords Proprietors, who would use it to pay the governor's salary and make a profit for themselves.

Within a short time, the Lords Proprietors decided that they had granted too much power to the Albemarle County people. In 1669, they placed a new frame of government called the Fundamental Constitutions in effect. The Fundamental Constitutions snatched some power away from the Assembly while increasing the Lords Proprietors' power. North Carolinians opposed this change. They were also angry that the Lords Proprietors raised the quitrents around this time.

For about 30 years the Proprietors tried to enforce the Fundamental Constitutions, but with great difficulty. Some people wouldn't pay the quitrents to the Proprietors. There were also rebellions against the proprietary government. One famous revolt, Culpeper's Rebellion, was aimed against Thomas Miller, who governed Albemarle County for a short time in 1677. North Carolinians called Miller a tyrant for taxing them, and for trying to deprive his enemies of the right to vote. Led by John Culpeper and several others, about 40 North Carolinians surrounded Miller's home in late 1677. They seized Miller and threw him in jail, then ran the government themselves for about two years with John Culpeper as acting governor. Culpeper's Rebellion was one of the first revolts by the American colonists against an unjust government.

Thomas Miller escaped from jail and sailed to England to complain about the North Carolina rebels. John Culpeper followed him to the mother country to present the rebels' side of the story. Although Culpeper could have been put to death for his actions, the Lords Proprietors sympathized with him and admitted that Miller had governed the colony badly.

Seth Sothell, the next man chosen by the Lords Proprietors to govern Albermarle County, was even more of a tyrant than Thomas Miller. On the way to North Carolina, Sothell was captured by pirates, who held him for about five years until he

Seth Sothell and his followers seizing the North Carolina government.

escaped. After finally reaching North Carolina in 1683, Sothell earned the people's hatred by taking bribes, seizing other people's land, and jailing his opponents. In 1689 the Albermarle County Assembly placed Sothell on trial for his misdeeds. He was thrown out of North Carolina and barred from ever holding office there again. When the Lords Proprietors heard about all this, they reacted much as they had toward Culpeper's Rebellion. They admitted that Seth Sothell had been a bad governor and even apologized to the people for having appointed him.

North Carolinians firmly opposed other governors besides Thomas Miller and Seth Sothell between 1664 and 1691. Then, starting in 1691, there was a change in government for North Carolina (as people were starting to call the Albermarle County region, even though officially there was no North Carolina or South Carolina as yet). By then the South Carolina region had its own governor, who ruled from Charleston, which was growing into a major colonial town. The

Charleston, South Carolina, in 1673

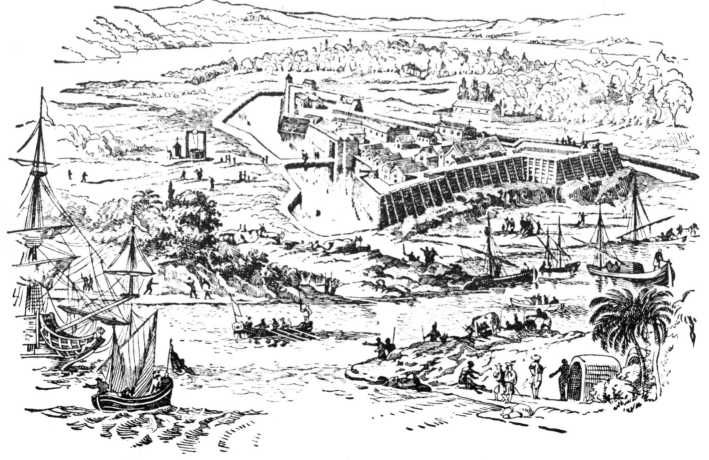

Proprietors decided that the governor of South Carolina would appoint a deputy governor to rule North Carolina.

What this meant was that the Lords Proprietors would no longer send governors from England to North Carolina. Instead, the governor at Charleston would appoint people who already lived in America to govern North Carolina. This system was a success. Between 1691 and 1705, five longtime Carolinians served as governor of North Carolina. For the most part they did a good job, helping to bring peace and growth to the colony. By 1705, the North Carolina region had around 12,000 people who were about to witness the creation of the colony's first towns.

A medal issued by the Lords Proprietors

"The Emigrants' Noonday Halt," a drawing by Sol Eytinge

Chapter V

Towns, Pirates, and Westward Expansion: 1705-1760

It [the government of North Carolina] is the mildest and best established Government in the World, and the Place where any Man may peaceably enjoy his own [life] without being invaded by another [person]. Rank and Superiority ever [give way] to Justice and Equity, which is the Golden Rule that every Government ought to be built upon.

From Lawson's History of North Carolina (1709) by John Lawson

By the early 1700s, North Carolinians had earned a reputation as a freedom-loving, tough people. Colonists elsewhere generally just complained about bad governors, but North Carolinians threw them out of office on their ears. Other colonies said "KEEP OUT" to certain people, but North Carolina welcomed nearly everyone. In other places the rich didn't socialize with the poor, but in North Carolina, where few people were wealthy, everyone mixed together at church services, court sessions, and other events.

Another way that North Carolina differed from the other colonies was that its people didn't build any towns for a long time. In Massachusetts, the Pilgrims who had arrived in 1620 had started building their first town, Plymouth, that very first winter. Likewise, South Carolinians had begun building the settlement that became Charleston very soon. But by 1700—115 years after Sir Walter Raleigh had first tried to start a town there—North Carolina still had no towns!

The Lords Proprietors were unhappy about this. Towns would make it easier for the colonists to conduct business—and for them to collect taxes.

Around 1704 or 1705 some of the French Protestants known as Huguenots moved out of Virginia in search of good land and more space. They settled near the Pamlico River in eastern North Carolina. By early 1706 an English surveyor named John Lawson had laid out the boundaries for North Carolina's first permanent European town at the place where the Huguenots had settled. It was named Bath, perhaps in honor of John Granville—the Earl of Bath, a city in England—who was one of the Lords Proprietors. North Carolina's oldest town never grew much larger than it was at that time. Today, about three centuries after it was built, Bath, North Carolina, is home to only about 200 people.

A few years later, in 1710, a land company in Switzerland sent a few hundred people, mostly German and Swiss, to America under the leadership of Baron Christopher von Graffenried and John Lawson. These people, who hoped to find religious and personal freedom and greater opportunities in America, settled about 40 miles southwest of Bath where the Neuse and the Trent rivers meet. There, under Lawson and Graffenried, they built North Carolina's second town. It was named New Bern in honor of Bern, Switzerland, Graffenried's birthplace. Around the time that New Bern celebrated its first birthday in 1711, disaster struck.

The Native Americans had been growing angrier at the North Carolina colonists, and with good reason. Like the settlers in the other colonies, the North Carolinians had pushed them off their lands and had treated them cruelly. By 1711 the Tuscarora felt that it was time to make a stand. With the help of several smaller tribes, the Tuscarora struck at the colonists with a fury.

The conflict began in early September of 1711 when John Lawson and Baron Graffenried went exploring with several friendly Indians and black slaves. Lawson and Graffenried wanted to know

Lawson and Graffenried surveying on the Neuse River

how far a boat could sail up the Neuse River, and how far west one had to travel before North Carolina became mountainous. They had been exploring for several days when they were captured by about 60 Indians. Lawson and Graffenried were taken to an Indian town where the Tuscarora chief King Hancock placed them on trial.

At first the Indians decided to release Lawson and Graffenried, but soon more Indians arrived who felt that the two white leaders should die. In the end, Graffenried was spared, perhaps because the Indians mistook him for North Carolina's Governor Edward Hyde, but John Lawson was tortured and killed. What made this especially tragic was that Lawson was one of the very few Englishmen who liked and respected the Indians.

Before releasing Graffenried, the Indians told him that they were about to attack the colonists in North Carolina. Graffenried made a deal with the Indians—if New Bern didn't take sides in the upcoming fight, the Indians would not attack the town.

At sunrise on September 22, 1711, hundreds of Indians attacked a number of North Carolina locations. They killed about 140 colonists and seized about 25 prisoners in these opening raids of what was called the Tuscarora War. True to their word, the Indians left New Bern unharmed. But after Graffenried returned home, some New Bern men who were angry about the deal he had made captured an Indian chief and burned him to death. As far as the Indians were concerned, New Bern was no longer protected. The Tuscarora then attacked colonists in the New Bern region, killing more people.

North Carolina was in a pitiful state by this time. Not only had many people been killed, but farms had been burned, crops and livestock had been destroyed, and the survivors were terrorized. Governor Hyde and North Carolina lawmakers asked Virginia for aid in fighting the Indians. When Virginia wasn't very helpful, North Carolina turned to its sister colony, South Carolina, for help. South Carolina organized an army of about 35 colonists and nearly 500 Yamasee—a South Carolina tribe that was friendly to the colonists but foes of the Tuscarora. Under Colonel John Barnwell, this army marched 300 miles from South Carolina to North Carolina's Neuse River region. Barnwell's army murdered many Tuscarora and destroyed several towns. Finally, in the spring of 1712, the Tuscarora made a peace treaty with Barnwell. The fighting was to end and the tribes were to move west of North Carolina's colonial settlements.

Right after this deal was made, some of Barnwell's Yamasee violated it by seizing a number of friends of the Tuscarora and selling them as slaves. The Tuscarora then resumed their attacks in mid-1712. This time about 35 white soldiers and 1,000 friendly Indians from South Carolina under Colonel James Moore were joined by about 200 North Carolinians. In March 1713, this very large colonial army crushed the Tuscarora in a tremendous battle fought near

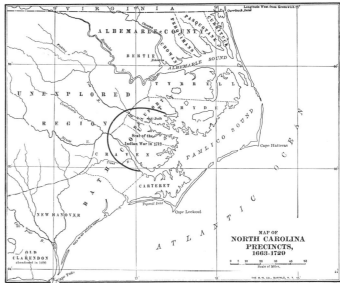

Conflicts with the Native Americans on the southwestern frontier frequently were caused by disputes over ownership of property.

present-day Snow Hill, North Carolina. About 1,000 Tuscarora were killed or captured in this battle, the last major conflict of the Tuscarora War. Only about 60 colonial troops were killed or wounded. A few years later, most of the remaining Tuscarora left North Carolina and joined their cousins, the Iroquois, in the New York Colony.

There was a big change in the Carolinas during the Tuscarora War. By the early 1700s people commonly spoke of North Carolina and South

Carolina as separate colonies, as we have been doing in this book to make things easier. For example, in *Lawson's History of North Carolina*, which was published in 1709, John Lawson described the region "commonly called North Carolina" as being separate from South Carolina. But technically there was still just one Carolina Colony, with the governor of the southern part appointing a deputy to govern the northern part. This ended in 1712, when North Carolina and South Carolina were made separate colonies, and the Lords Proprietors began appointing North Carolina's governors themselves.

Medal struck in 1736 to commemorate the separation of North and South Carolina

Also around the time of the Tuscarora War, North Carolina was plagued by pirates. These pirates, including several females, robbed ships at sea. The ship owners and the merchants and wealthy planters who shipped goods were the big losers when the pirates struck, but many other people profited. Private citizens were able to buy goods from pirates for less than the usual cost, much as some people buy stolen goods today. Tavern owners and shopkeepers liked the way the pirates freely spent their gold and silver. Many dishonest lawmakers ignored the pirates or even became friendly with them in exchange for bribes they were paid by the buccaneers.

In the early 1700s the North Carolina shore was one of the world's main pirate hideouts. The colony was home to few of the ship owners, merchants, and wealthy planters who were hurt by piracy. And, physically, North Carolina was perfect. Pirate ships could lurk around the islands and sandbars of the Outer Banks. Then when a merchant ship passed, the pirates could raise the Jolly Roger (their skull-and-crossbones flag) and rob the vessel. If chased, the pirate ships could hide in any one of a thousand remote spots along North Carolina's 300-mile coastline. The colony also had its share of dishonest officials who would look the other way if given enough gold and silver.

Blackbeard, with smoking matches under his hat

The most famous pirate associated with North Carolina was known as Blackbeard, because of the long black beard that he braided and tied with colored ribbons. Blackbeard made himself look as terrifying as possible, not only to scare his victims but to keep his men in line. His belts and holsters were filled with guns, knives, and swords. Before going into battle, he lit slow-burning matches and stuck them under his hat, so that smoke seemed to be coming out of his ears. When people saw the black-bearded man with the smoking head and the arsenal of weapons, they were usually quick to surrender!

Blackbeard's ships, the *Queen Anne's Revenge* and the *Adventure*, robbed many vessels along the coasts of the Carolinas, Virginia, and Delaware. His headquarters were at Bath, North Carolina, where Charles Eden, who governed North Carolina from 1714 to 1722, had a home. Blackbeard befriended Governor Eden (perhaps by paying him off), and even lived for a time in a home across the creek from the governor. It was said that an underground tunnel led from the creek to the governor's house, so that Blackbeard could secretly send Eden a share of the stolen loot.

Stede Bonnet (?–1718), a former major in the British army, was another of the pirates who sailed along the North Carolina shore. It was said that Bonnet was a wealthy planter on the British-ruled island of Barbados when he turned pirate to escape his wife's nasty temper. By 1718, his headquarters were the lower part of the Cape Fear River in southeastern North Carolina. Although he was called the "Gentleman Pirate," Bonnet could be very cruel. He sometimes killed his victims by making them "walk the plank" (jump into the ocean), a practice that is shown in many movies but that few pirates actually used.

By 1718, the ship owners, rich planters, and merchants who suffered most from piracy were growing in numbers in Virginia and the Carolinas—particularly in South Carolina—and many of these people wanted to put a stop to piracy in the region. Governor Eden wouldn't oppose the pirates, so the governors of South Carolina and Virginia dealt with the problem.

South Carolina's Governor Robert Johnson sent Colonel William Rhett out pirate hunting in 1718. That fall, Rhett fought a sea battle with Stede Bonnet at the mouth of Cape Fear River in North Carolina. The "Gentleman Pirate" was captured and taken to Charleston, South Carolina, where he was hanged in late 1718. Around the same time, about 50 other pirates, including many of Bonnet's men, were also hanged in the South Carolina capital.

In late 1718, Virginia Governor Alexander Spotswood sent out two ships under Lieutenant Robert Maynard of the British navy to capture Blackbeard. Maynard found Blackbeard near one of his favorite haunts—Ocracoke Inlet along North Carolina's Outer Banks. On November 22, 1718, Blackbeard's and Maynard's men fought a tremendous sea battle in which there were a number of deaths on both sides. Finally, Maynard and Blackbeard faced each other and both men fired their guns. Blackbeard was shot and

Alexander Spotswood

85

Blackbeard's head hanging from the bow of a ship

wounded, but kept on fighting. The famous pirate was about to kill Maynard with his cutlass when a British sailor suddenly slit Blackbeard's throat. Maynard then cut off Blackbeard's head and hung it from his ship as proof that the legendary pirate was really dead.

About ten of Blackbeard's men died in this battle. The remaining fourteen were taken to Virginia where they were tried and then hanged. The deaths of Blackbeard, Stede Bonnet, and dozens of other pirates in 1718 marked the end of major piracy in North Carolina.

The decline of piracy meant that merchants could ship goods in and out of the Carolinas and Virginia with less fear of theft. Among the main items that North Carolina shipped to England during the 1700s were "naval stores"—tar, turpentine, and other products from pine trees that were used to build and repair ships. During the 1700s, North Carolina provided about seventy percent of the tar and over half the turpentine sent to England by the thirteen colonies. In fact, North Carolina led the world in producing naval stores for 150 years between 1720 and 1870. Other products that merchants shipped out of North Carolina during the 1700s included tobacco, which went mainly to England, and

A North Carolina
turpentine distillery

timber and food, which went mainly to the islands off Florida that belonged to England.

It was tragic for the Tuscarora that most of them had left North Carolina by the early 1720s, but it was good news for the colonists. Settlers moved onto what had been Tuscarora lands, and also onto the lands of other tribes who were crowded out of North Carolina. Soon after major fighting in the Tuscarora War ended in 1713, several more towns besides Bath and New Bern were built along the North Carolina coast. Around 1713 North Carolina's third town—Beaufort—was established about 40 miles southeast of New Bern. In its early years Beaufort was settled by French, Scottish, Irish, German, and Swedish people, as well as those of English backgrounds. Around 1714 a town was begun near the colony's northeastern corner. It was named Edenton for Charles Eden, the governor who was Blackbeard's friend. Brunswick was founded about 1726 near the mouth of the Cape Fear River in southeastern North Carolina, and in about 1733, Wilmington was settled nearby.

By 1729, when North Carolina had been a proprietary colony for nearly seventy years, many people were ready for a change in government. The Lords Proprietors had never earned enough money from North Carolina to make up for all the headaches of running the colony. For their part, North Carolinians had never been very happy under proprietary rule. In 1729 all of the current Proprietors but one sold their shares in North Carolina to King George II, and North Carolina was placed under the king's rule as a royal colony. Under this new system, the king appointed North Carolina's governors.

The first settlers
clearing the land

The change to royal colony status was the shot in the arm that North Carolina needed. For one thing, it meant more security, because the king was more protective of colonies under his direct rule than of those run by proprietors. Between 1730 and 1760, North Carolina enjoyed tremendous population growth as people moved there from Europe and from other American colonies. During those thirty years, North Carolina's population soared from about 30,000 to about 110,000 people. Only Delaware, Pennsylvania, and New Hampshire had a similar population increase through those years.

A clearing and log cabin on the frontier

The people who came to North Carolina gradually moved westward from the seacoast. In the 1730s, people from Scotland began arriving in North Carolina. In 1739, the Scots settled in an area about 100 miles from the ocean that became Fayetteville, North Carolina. By the late 1700s, about 15 out of every 100 North Carolinians were of Scottish origin. The only colonies with as large a proportion of Scots were Georgia and South Carolina. Several North Carolina place names, including Scotland County and the town of Scotland Neck, honor the early Scottish settlers.

Large numbers of German settlers also came to

North Carolina. One group were Moravians, a Protestant religious sect from Germany. In 1753 a band of Moravians walked about 500 miles from Bethlehem, Pennsylvania, to northwestern North Carolina in about a month! During the 1750s and 1760s the Moravians founded several towns in northwestern North Carolina, including the settlement that grew into the city of Winston-Salem.

The Scotch-Irish were another group that settled the North Carolina frontier. Hundreds of years ago, England began to conquer Ireland, an island country a short way to its west. The English, who were Protestants, killed Irish Catholic priests and pushed many Irish Catholics off their lands. In their place the English settled many Protestants from Scotland. Because they came from Scotland but lived in Ireland, these people became known as the Scotch-Irish. Between the 1730s and the 1770s, about 65,000 Scotch-Irish people settled in the North Carolina interior. Around 1748 some of them settled in the area that grew into Charlotte, North Carolina. Located in far southern North Carolina near the South Carolina line, Charlotte today is the largest city in the Carolinas.

Colonial mountaineers

By 1760 English, German, Scottish, Scotch-Irish, and other people had populated every part of what is now North Carolina except the mountains in the west. This area was still a Cherokee stronghold—and would remain so until the 1830s, when most of the Cherokee were pushed out of North Carolina.

The frontier people in central and western North Carolina dressed in buckskin, walked around with their rifles, and built log cabins. They were what we might call "real Daniel Boone types" during the mid-1700s. That was fitting because North Carolina was home to the real Daniel Boone for many years!

JOHN LAWSON (?–1711)

John Lawson was born somewhere in England during the late 1600s. We know nothing of his life until the year 1700, when he decided to leave England and see the world. Lawson apparently was going to Rome, Italy, when he met a man who had traveled widely. This man convinced Lawson that Carolina was the best place in the world for him to visit.

In the early fall of 1700 Lawson reached Charleston, South Carolina. After a time, he moved to North Carolina, where by 1706 he had helped to found Bath, the colony's first permanent European town. Lawson loved North Carolina and spent a lot of time visiting its tribes and exploring its countryside. While living in North Carolina, he wrote a book about the colony. By 1709, *Lawson's History of North Carolina* was finished and he was back in England overseeing its publication.

Much of *Lawson's History* describes the Indians of North Carolina. Lawson was one of only a handful of American colonists who admired the Native Americans. He wrote that they were "really better to us than we are to them" and complained about the colonists' cruelty toward the Native Americans. Lawson also noted that, crowded though they were, their wigwams never smelled bad. If that many English people were crowded together, he added, "We should be poisoned with our own Nastiness, which confirms these Indians to be, as they really are, some of the sweetest people in the World."

Among the other highlights of Lawson's book are his wonderful descriptions of North Carolina wildlife. He explained that alligators in North Carolina sometimes grew more than 17 feet in length. He described a gorgeous green, orange, and yellow bird called the Carolina parakeet—a bird none of us will ever see because it has since been wiped out. And he related that the Native Americans and the colonists made pets of some animals that are rarely tamed today, including skunks, beavers, green snakes, mockingbirds, cardinals, cranes, raccoons, and squirrels.

Around the time of Lawson's visit to England, the Lords Proprietors made him chief surveyor of North Carolina. In connection with this post, Lawson was to help Baron Christopher von Graffenried of Switzerland settle a large number of German and Swiss people in North Carolina. Lawson returned to North Carolina with a few hundred settlers in early 1710, and helped them build New Bern, North Carolina's second town.

Lawson had but a short time to live after this. In early September 1711, he was captured and killed by Indians in an incident that started the Tuscarora War. Although Lawson had been friendly with the Indians, they may have killed him because of this town-building, or out of their general hatred for white people. John Lawson's fascinating book has been republished several times since 1709 and still can be found in some libraries.

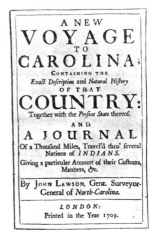

Title page of John Lawson's book

BLACKBEARD (About 1680?–1718)

Blackbeard

Little is known about the famous pirate Blackbeard except for the last few years of his life. He is thought to have been born in either Bristol, England, or on the British-ruled island of Jamaica. We are not sure of Blackbeard's real name. Although he was known as Edward Teach, pirates commonly used false names to protect their families, so this may not have been his real name. One clue about his background was that he could read and write well, implying that he probably came from a rather well-to-do family.

During Queen Anne's War (1702–1713), Teach worked out of Jamaica as a privateer for England. Privateers were the commanders of private ships hired by the government in wartime to attack enemy ships. Teach had great success in his attacks on French and Spanish ships. When the war against France and Spain ended, many of the privateers, including Teach, turned to piracy.

Around 1716, Teach went to work for the well-known pirate Benjamin Hornigold, who made his headquarters at the town of Nassau in the Bahama Islands. Teach helped Hornigold capture ships around the Bahamas and was soon rewarded with his own vessel. After equipping it with seventy men and six cannons, Teach robbed so many ships in so short a time that he became a legendary figure even to other pirates. In 1717, Teach broke away from Hornigold and set out on his own. For the last year or so of his life he concentrated on robbing ships along and near the Carolina coast.

Teach wanted to be known as the world's most wicked pirate so that his victims would surrender at the sight of him, and he wouldn't have to fight. About the time that he broke away from Hornigold, he grew his famous long black beard, adopted the name Blackbeard, and began sticking slow-burning matches under his hat so that his head appeared to be smoking. It was said that Blackbeard didn't harm people who turned over their valuables when he robbed their ships. But someone who didn't hand over a diamond ring might lose the ring *and* the finger it was on.

From time to time, the British kings and queens offered pardons to pirates who promised to become honest men. In early 1718 Blackbeard sailed to Bath, North Carolina, where he took the vow to give up piracy. He was pardoned for his past misdeeds and lived for a few months near Governor Charles Eden in Bath. He even married a 16-year-old girl in Bath who was said to be his fourteenth wife! Apparently all or most of the earlier marriages had been performed on shipboard and weren't legal.

Blackbeard soon broke his promise and continued to sail out from his hiding place at Ocracoke Inlet to rob ships. He seems to have done this with the blessing of Governor Eden. Finally in late 1718 Governor

Alexander Spotswood of Virginia sent out the expedition that tracked down and killed Blackbeard in a sea battle near Ocracoke Inlet.

The Blackbeard legend continued to grow after his death. People claimed that after Blackbeard's headless body was thrown into the water, it swam about for quite a while before sinking! And for many years, when people along the North Carolina coast saw unidentified lights, they claimed that it was Blackbeard with a lantern looking for his head.

DANIEL BOONE (1734–1820)

Daniel Boone

Daniel Boone was born into a Quaker family near present-day Reading, Pennsylvania. From his boyhood, Daniel deeply loved the outdoors. When his family attended Quaker religious meetings, Daniel stayed as long as his mother held his hand. The moment she let go, he ran out the door to play in the woods. Daniel wasn't as peaceful as Quakers were supposed to be, either. When non-Quakers laughed at his family and friends for wearing plain clothes and saying "thee" and "thou," he sometimes corrected their ways with his fists.

Compared to his brothers, sisters, and cousins, Daniel had little education. His family couldn't get him to stay inside long enough to teach him more than a little reading and writing. But when it came to the outdoors, he was a great student. His favorite teachers were the Indians, who taught him such skills as how to make a fire with sticks and how to walk through the woods without leaving a trail. Daniel practiced so much with his bow and arrow and his rifle that by the age of thirteen he was an expert with both of them. Once when Daniel and some friends were playing near a riverbank, they stumbled upon a wildcat. His friends ran away, but just as the wildcat sprang at him, Daniel shot it dead.

Daniel's father let his children marry non-Quakers, which led to quarrels with other Quakers. In the spring of 1748, Daniel's father was kicked out of the local Quaker group. The Boones then decided to move south. They packed their goods into wagons and left their Pennsylvania home on the first day of May, 1750. Fifteen-year-old Daniel walked ahead of the wagons with his long rifle in his arms. After a trip of about 500 miles, the family settled along western North Carolina's Yadkin River in 1751. The Boones lived in a cave their first winter in North Carolina before building a cabin in the spring. Daniel lived in several places in North Carolina over the next few years.

Daniel Boone became known for his marksmanship out on the North Carolina frontier. Besides bringing wild game home for his family, he won one shooting match after another. People even joked that he could lick a tick—shoot a bug—off a bear's nose at 300 feet. Because of these stories, Daniel named his rifle Tick-Licker.

In 1755, during the French and Indian War, 21-year-old Daniel Boone joined the forces of British General Edward Braddock, which were about to attack the enemy in western Pennsylvania. Daniel worked as a wagon driver and blacksmith for Braddock, but he would have been better used as a soldier. Braddock's forces were smashed at the Battle of the Wilderness, which was fought in July 1755. More than half the British troops were killed or wounded in this battle but Boone was not harmed.

About a year later, Daniel married 16-year-old Rebecca Bryan. The couple had ten children and remained married for more than 56 years until Rebecca died in 1813. Often during those years Rebecca had to care for the family alone while Daniel was out hunting, exploring, or building new settlements.

While he was with Braddock, Daniel had heard about a beautiful land called Kentucky. Between 1767 and 1771 Boone made two long trips into Kentucky to hunt for furs and explore. He was the most famous of a small group of men who were called "long hunters" because they spent long periods of time in the wilderness. Boone had many adventures while out hunting. It was said that once when he was trapped by hostile Indians on a cliff he saved himself by leaping a great distance into a tree. Unfortunately, all the furs Daniel had gathered on his second "long hunt" were stolen. He returned to his family poor—but with a yearning for Kentucky.

In 1773 Boone sold his North Carolina farm and led his family and a few other North Carolinians toward Kentucky. On the way, they were attacked by Indians. Several people, including Daniel and Rebecca's oldest son, James, were killed, and the survivors had to turn back. Still, Daniel wouldn't give up his dream of moving to Kentucky. Two years later, in 1775, he helped build the Wilderness Road linking Virginia to Kentucky. Thousands of pioneers took this trail west over the next few years. Also in 1775, Daniel founded Boonesborough (near present-day Lexington), one of Kentucky's first white settlements. Soon, Daniel brought his family to live in Boonesborough.

Realizing that the white people wanted Kentucky, the Indians made several attacks on Boonesborough. Once they kidnapped three girls including Daniel's daughter, Jemima. Daniel tracked the girls down and freed them during a fight with the Indians. Then in February 1778, Daniel was out gathering salt and hunting when he was captured by Shawnee. Instead of killing him, Chief Blackfish adopted Daniel. For several months, Daniel dressed and lived like a Shawnee. In fact, he and his Shawnee "family" grew to love each other very much. But finally, after

Daniel Boone rescues his daughter and her friends.

hearing that the Indians were about to attack Boonesborough, Daniel escaped. He then made one of the most amazing journeys in the history of frontier America, hiking 160 miles through the wilderness in about four days with hundreds of warriors trailing him. He reached Boonesborough in time to help save it from a major Indian attack.

Helping to settle Kentucky was Daniel Boone's great contribution to America, but he couldn't live out his days there. Because of his distaste for lawyers and paperwork, Daniel never obtained proper title to his Kentucky lands, and lost them as a result. Around 1788 he moved to what is now West Virginia and about ten years later he moved to Missouri, where he served as a judge and public official for several years. In his eighties, Daniel made a trip to the Yellowstone River region about 1,000 miles northwest of his Missouri home. He was thinking about visiting California when he died in Missouri a few weeks before his eighty-sixth birthday. Among the many places that have been named for the nation's most famous pioneer are the town of Boone in northwestern North Carolina and Boone County in Kentucky.

"Clearing Up a Farm," a drawing by R. E. Robinson

Chapter VI

Daily Life in the 1760s

This province [North Carolina] is settling faster than any on the continent. Last autumn and winter, upwards of one thousand wagons passed through Salisbury [a town in western North Carolina] with families from the northward, to settle in this province chiefly.

> *Arthur Dobbs, North Carolina's governor from 1754 to 1765, writing about the colony in 1766*

With 110,000 people, North Carolina was average in population among the thirteen colonies as of 1760. North Carolina had more people than six colonies, and fewer people than six colonies. Between 1760 and 1770, North Carolina's population nearly doubled to about 200,000 people, moving it up to fifth place in the colonial population derby. Only Virginia gained more people during those ten years.

People moved to North Carolina because it offered plenty of farmland, a warm climate, and more freedom than most colonies. Thousands of the newcomers settled in the frontier areas of central and western North Carolina. A newspaper report of the late 1760s had this to say about North Carolina: "There is scarce any history either ancient or modern, which affords an account of such a rapid and sudden increase of inhabitants in a back frontier country, as that of North Carolina."

Few colonies had as much human variety as North Carolina. About two-thirds of all North Carolinians were of English background, but the colony also had many people of African, Scottish, Irish, Scotch-Irish, German, French, Dutch, Swedish, and Welsh backgrounds. And there were people of many different faiths in the colony including Church of Englanders, Quakers, Lutherans, Moravians, Baptists, Methodists, and Presbyterians.

Although North Carolina had a few towns by 1760, all of them were small by modern standards. The two largest towns—New Bern and Wilmington —had a few hundred people. The typical town, however, consisted of a couple of dirt roads on which stood a courthouse, a jail, a tavern, a store or two, some houses, and several other buildings. The towns had a rural look. Wagons filled with farm goods moved slowly along the roads. Chickens flew about, and hogs and cattle roamed

Street scene in a colonial town

the streets as people conducted their business.

In 1760 most North Carolinians lived on farms scattered across the countryside. About 95 out of every 100 North Carolinians worked at farming or a related activity back then. Among their main crops were corn, tobacco, wheat, peas, beans, barley, oats, rye, and rice.

A few North Carolinians owned plantations that covered about 10,000 acres, or about 16 square miles. A very few owned plantations of up to about 50,000 acres, or about 80 square miles. Orton Plantation, near Wilmington, which was the home of "King" Roger Moore and his family, was a well-known North Carolina plantation of the 1700s. Other large plantations included Lilliput (also near Wilmington) and Old Town Plantation in Edgecombe County.

Rich planters had costly coaches and horses.

Compared to other North Carolinians, the rich planters and their families enjoyed an easy life. Slaves grew their tobacco and other crops, dressed them in their wigs and silver-buckled shoes, and cooked and served their meals. What feasts those meals often were! When company came, the slaves might prepare roast turkey, beef, ham, goose, and duck. Drinks included wines from across the Atlantic Ocean and alcoholic punches. Dessert might be cheesecake, minced pie, and tarts.

The children of the wealthy were the best-educated young people in the colony. North Carolina's first known schoolteacher, Charles Griffin, opened a school near the northeastern corner of the colony in 1705. Few other schools were founded until the 1760s when many new schools and academies opened. For example, Tate's Academy in Wilmington opened in 1760, and academies appeared later in New Bern and Edenton. North Carolina's best-known academy, the "Log College," was founded at present-day Greensboro in 1767 by the Reverend David Caldwell. A large school for its time with about fifty students yearly, the "Log College" lasted into the early 1800s. Children of wealthy families who didn't attend a school or academy were often taught at home by private tutors. North Carolina had no colleges in the 1760s. A few wealthy young men (females weren't allowed to attend college back then) went to colleges in other colonies and in England and Scotland.

The slaves who worked in the tobacco and rice fields lived a much different kind of life than their masters. By 1760, about 30,000 North Carolinians —more than a quarter of the population—were slaves. The great majority of the slaves lived in the eastern part of the colony. Frontier families generally couldn't afford slaves and did their own farming.

The slaves—or their ancestors—had been taken from Africa to America in slave ships. The slaves were kept in chains during the ocean crossing so that they couldn't revolt or drown themselves. About a fifth of the slaves died of disease on the way to America and were buried at sea.

A slave mother and her child at an auction

A few African slaves were landed in Wilmington and Bath, North Carolina, but most of North Carolina's slaves were bought from slave dealers in South Carolina and Virginia. Regardless of where it was held, a slave auction was a tragic event for the Africans. Not only did they lose their freedom, in many cases their families were ripped apart. The father might be bought by a planter in one part of North Carolina, and the mother and children by planters who lived hundreds of miles away. A white man who saw a slave auction in Wilmington, North Carolina, in the 1770s wrote: "A [slave mother] clung to a little daughter, and implored, with the most agonizing supplication, that they might not be separated." The mother was pleading because she knew she might never see her little girl again if they were sold separately. As she had feared, they were bought by different masters.

Things didn't get better for the slaves once they reached their master's home. They worked from sunrise to sunset at such jobs as growing tobacco and rice, tending livestock, and cooking meals for their masters in the "big house." The slave quarters were often ramshackle huts with dirt floors. Most masters fed their slaves as cheaply as possible on hominy, old bacon, fat from meat,

Slaves loading rice at a riverside plantation

skimmed milk, and salted fish. Slaves were given little clothing. Some weren't given *any* clothing until they were thirteen or fourteen years old.

The masters feared that if their slaves read books about human rights or sent letters to each other, they might revolt. This was one reason why slaves were not taught to read or write. As a result, we lack written descriptions of what it was like to be a slave in colonial North Carolina. However, after the slaves were freed in the 1860s, some of them explained what slavery had been like. The following descriptions by two former slaves who grew up in North Carolina in the mid-1800s would also hold true for the 1760s:

> Our cabins were built of poles and had stick-and-dirt chimneys, one door, and one little window at the back end of the cabin. Some of the houses had dirt floors. Our clothing was poor and homemade.
>
> Many of the slaves went bareheaded and barefooted. Some wore rags around their heads, and some wore bonnets. We had poor food, and the young slaves were fed out of troughs [a container used to feed animals]. The food was put in a trough, and the little [children] gathered around and ate. The children were looked after by the old slave women who were unable to work in the fields, while the mothers of the babies worked. The women plowed and did other work as the men did. No books or learning of any kind were allowed. No prayer meetings were allowed, but we sometimes went to the white folks' church. They told us to obey our masters and be obedient at all times.
>
> Conditions and rules were bad and the punishments were severe. . . . Some masters acted like savages. In some instances slaves were burned at the stake. Families were torn apart by selling. Mothers were sold from their children. Children were sold from their mothers, and the father was not considered in any way as a family part.

Because of their fear of a slave revolt, North Carolinians passed special laws concerning slaves during colonial times. By the 1760s, the slaves were governed by a number of harsh laws. For example, slaves found away from home without a written pass could be whipped. Three or more slaves who planned a rebellion were to be killed. Yet a planter could murder a slave and not be punished, because slaves were considered property, much like farm animals. Not until 1774 did North Carolina consider the killing of slaves to be murder.

Although runaway slaves who were caught were severely beaten, many slaves fled anyway. North Carolina newspapers (the colony's first newspaper had been founded at New Bern in 1751) ran many ads for runaway slaves. The following ad appeared on July 10, 1765, in the *North Carolina Gazette* published in Wilmington:

> *Ran away on Thursday Night last, a Negro Fellow called Boston; about Forty Years of Age; middle-sized; and rather thin than corpulent; stoops a little in his walk, and speaks fast: Had on when he run away, a blue Jacket. . . . Any person who apprehends said Negro, and brings him to the Subscriber in Wilmington, shall have Twenty Shillings Reward.*
> *George Parker*

Some runaways chose to kill themselves rather than return to a life of slavery. Court records from 1766 tell of a runaway slave from the Wilmington region who "upon being [captured] jumped into the river and drowned himself."

A log-cabin homestead on the frontier

By the 1760s, North Carolina was also home to several thousand free African Americans, many of whom had been released from slavery by the terms of their masters' wills. Some freed slaves saved money on their jobs, bought friends and relatives who were slaves, and then freed them. It was dangerous for them to stay in North Carolina, though. They risked being kidnapped and sold back into slavery.

Most North Carolinians of the 1760s were neither slaves nor rich planters, but people who had to work hard to feed and dress their families. The typical North Carolina family of the 1760s lived in a wooden house that they had built themselves. Perhaps they owned a few metal spoons and store-bought clothes, but they generally made most of their own household goods, especially if they lived on the frontier. They made beds, tables, chairs, and even spoons out of wood. Dried gourds were used as drinking cups. Animal fat was made into candles, and fireplace ashes were used to make soap. Mothers and daughters sewed most of the family's clothes out of deerskin or cloth.

These average North Carolinians ate much better than the slaves, but not as well as the rich planters. They enjoyed ham, pork, corn bread, corn stews, and potatoes produced on their own farms. Fish and venison added to their diet. Coffee, tea, corn beer, persimmon beer, potato brandy, and dandelion wine were popular drinks.

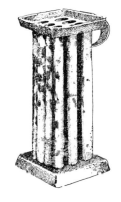

A mold for making candles

A colonial home, with a cooking pot over the fire and a spinning wheel

North Carolina did not begin a public-school system until the 1840s, more than half a century after colonial times ended. There were some church schools and private schools for less-wealthy North Carolinians in the 1760s, but thousands of children never went to school a day in their lives. Many young North Carolinians never even learned how to write their names.

Whether they were rich planters, slaves, or poor farmers, the North Carolinians of the 1760s knew how to have fun. Wealthy people held balls where they danced formally. Poorer folks held "frolics" at which they danced to the music of a fiddle or bagpipes. Slaves were often allowed to have Saturday night "frolics," too. It was a custom

Young people frolicking at a corn-shucking bee

among North Carolina slaves and some white people to hold a "frolic" in honor of a person who had just died.

Frontier people gathered for "house-raisings." These were get-togethers at which neighbors helped new families build their cabins. Once the home was up, everyone enjoyed dancing, games, and wrestling contests. In the fall, young people held "corn-shucking bees." They sat around in a circle and talked as they husked the corn. Meanwhile, their mothers might be holding a "quilting bee."

Women and girls were excluded from sports back in the 1760s. Among North Carolina men and boys, horse racing was a passion. Some masters even allowed their slaves to hold horse races. Also popular was the brutal "sport" of cockfighting, in which two fighting roosters were placed in a pit where they battled until one of them was dead. Wrestling and shooting matches were favorite sports among frontiersmen. Cards, billiards, and games using dice were played in North Carolina's taverns.

Women, slaves, and the poorer male colonists were excluded from politics. Only white men and free black men who owned a certain amount of land or money could vote. But many North

Man with a gun. Shooting matches were popular.

Carolinians were troubled by the political situation of the 1760s.

For one thing, western North Carolinians were arguing with the easterners. By the 1760s, the western part of the colony was catching up to the east in population, yet it had far fewer representatives in the North Carolina legislature than the east did. The easterners used cunning methods to keep control of the government. As is true of nearly all states today, colonial North Carolina was divided into governmental units called counties. Each county sent representatives to the legislature. The easterners kept dividing up their region into new counties, so that they would have more and more representatives. Yet they were slow to create new counties in the west. And that wasn't the westerners' only complaint.

By 1766, North Carolina's colonial capital had been moved many times. It had been located at Edenton, New Bern, Wilmington, Bath, and other places chosen by the North Carolina governors. In 1766, the legislature named New Bern as the fixed capital. Located in the far eastern part of the colony, New Bern was hard for western lawmakers to reach. Also in 1766, the legislature ordered that a huge home for the governor be built in New Bern. Called Tryon's Palace (for William Tryon, royal governor between 1765 and 1771), this mansion was paid for by taxes imposed on people throughout the colony. Westerners hated having to pay for a governor's palace that few of them would ever see. They also considered it a terrible waste of money, especially since many of them were very poor.

Another of the westerners' complaints was that quite a few of their local officials, including many judges and sheriffs, were dishonest men who had been appointed by Governor Tryon. These men often cheated and stole from the westerners. Tryon himself figured that crooked county sheriffs had stolen more than half the tax money that was owed the North Carolina government between 1754 and 1767. Even by colonial standards, when lawmakers were generally less honest than they are today, there was a tremendous amount of thievery in North Carolina.

While North Carolinians argued with each other, England was also causing problems for all thirteen colonies. The mother country needed money, and in the 1760s, it began taxing the Americans to obtain it. This infuriated the colonists. A few years later, the regional trouble in North Carolina and the conflicts with England over taxes boiled over into war.

Governor Tryon and the Regulators

Chapter VII

Regulators and Revolutionaries: 1764-1783

We will resist it to the death!

> *North Carolina lawmaker John Ashe,*
> *explaining his colony's reaction to the*
> *Stamp Act of 1765*

THE WAR OF THE REGULATION

Thousands of western North Carolinians were enraged over their small representation in the legislature, the taxes they paid for Tryon's Palace, and crooked officials in the east. In 1768, they created a group called the Regulators that was dedicated to obtaining justice for the westerners. The group's name reflected its two purposes. The westerners wanted more of a say in regulating their own affairs, and they hoped to regulate the dishonest lawmakers in their midst.

Under their leaders—Herman Husband, Rednap Howell, and James Hunter—the Regulators were peaceful at first. They passed out leaflets at churches and courts, and sent petitions to Governor Tryon and the North Carolina legislature. But when little was done to meet their demands, the Regulators attacked officials in several towns. In September 1770, Regulators seized control of the court in Hillsborough, North Carolina, beat up local officials, and destroyed their property.

Reports of the "Hillsborough Riot" and rumors that the Regulators planned to march on the legislature at New Bern reached Governor Tryon. In the spring of 1771, Governor Tryon raised about 1,500 emergency troops called militiamen, some two-thirds of whom were from the east. The governor led them to Great Alamance Creek in Alamance County, west of Hillsborough. Meanwhile, the Regulators raised about 2,000 men of their own, but only about half of them had guns. On May 16, 1771, the Regulators met the militiamen at Great Alamance Creek and asked to talk to the governor. However, Tryon refused to meet with the Regulators and instead gave them one hour to lay down their guns and head home. Reportedly, the Regulators then said they were prepared to fight "Billy Tryon."

A number of the Regulators seem to have felt that Tryon would give in to their demands at the last second. It was said that some of them wrestled and played games during the hour. But when the

Governor Tryon orders his troops to fire upon the Regulators.

sixty minutes were up, Governor Tryon did not back down. "Fire! Fire!" he yelled. At first, his astonished troops refused to fire on their fellow North Carolinians. "Fire on them or fire on me!" the raging Tryon screamed. The next moment the militiamen opened fire on the Regulators.

Many of the Regulators who had guns fired back, but at the end of the two-hour battle, the Regulators fled. It appears that each side had about ten men killed, but that the Regulators had many wounded. Six Regulators were captured and tried for treason (serious crimes against the government), and then hanged.

The Battle of Alamance marked the end of the "War of the Regulation." Governor Tryon offered to pardon all Regulators who laid down their weapons and acknowledged him as the head of government. About 6,500 Regulators did this, but several thousand others chose to leave instead. Many of them went to Tennessee, which then belonged to North Carolina.

Several historians have called the Battle of Alamance the first battle of the Revolutionary War, which the Americans fought to break free from England. It is true that the Regulators rebelled against authority, much as the American patriots did in the Revolution. It also appears that most of the Regulators became revolutionaries. But today the Regulation movement is generally considered separate from the American Revolution. The Regulators and the revolutionaries had two different enemies. The Regulators rebelled against the officials from eastern North Carolina, while the revolutionaries rebelled against the mother country—England.

THE REVOLUTIONARY WAR

England wasn't the only nation that wanted to control North America. France and Spain also hoped to rule the continent. France ruled part of

Canada, which it called *New France*, to the north of England's thirteen colonies and also the huge Louisiana territory to the west of the thirteen colonies. Spain ruled Florida, to the south of the thirteen colonies.

Between 1689 and 1763, England fought several wars against France and Spain for control of North America. The Americans, including many North Carolinians, helped England fight these colonial wars by providing troops and money.

English and Spanish forces fought the War of Jenkins' Ear from 1739 to 1744. It was given this strange name because it began after the Spanish reportedly cut off the ear of an English sea captain named Robert Jenkins. In 1741, North Carolina provided about 400 men for a British attack on the Spanish at Cartagena in what is now Colombia, South America. This attack failed, resulting in the deaths of most of the North Carolinians and thousands of British troops.

For a time, it appeared that Spain might win the War of Jenkins' Ear and seize Georgia and the Carolinas. However, England's colonial forces smashed the Spanish at the Battle of Bloody Marsh in Georgia in the summer of 1742. Although Spain made several minor attacks on such North Carolina coastal towns as Beaufort and Brunswick in 1747–1748, the English victory at Bloody Marsh meant that Spain wouldn't be taking over Georgia and the Carolinas.

England and France fought four colonial wars, which were:

King William's War (1689–1697)

Queen Anne's War (1702–1713); Spain also fought England in this war

King George's War (1744–1748)

The French and Indian War (1754–1763)

The clash with France wasn't settled until the French and Indian War. Hundreds of North Carolinians took part in this war, which earned

George Washington leading British troops in an attack on a French encampment in the French and Indian War.

its name from the fact that many Native Americans helped the French fight the English and the American colonists. In 1760, near the end of the French and Indian War, North Carolina's Hugh Waddell and his men won an important victory over the Cherokee in the western part of the colony. The next year, the Cherokee signed a treaty in which they gave up land in far western North Carolina to the white settlers.

By winning the French and Indian War in 1763, England established itself as the ruling force in North America. But England had built up a huge national debt during the war. In order to pay its debts, the English lawmaking body called Parliament decided that the Americans should shoulder some of the load. Between 1764 and 1773, Parliament passed a number of laws ordering the colonists to pay taxes on such items as sugar, tea, and newspapers.

The Americans despised these taxes. One tax law they especially hated was the Stamp Act of 1765. It directed them to buy tax stamps and place them on newspapers and legal papers. From Maine to Georgia, Americans cried, "Taxation without representation is tyranny." This meant that since they weren't allowed to serve in

Parliament, the English government had no right to tax them.

Throughout the thirteen colonies, groups calling themselves Sons of Liberty protested the Stamp Act. The Sons of Liberty in Boston, Massachusetts, were the most violent. They wrecked buildings belonging to British officials and beat up Americans who did business with Britain. After learning about the Stamp Act in mid-1765, several North Carolinians including

A tax stamp (top left). A popular newspaper heading of the time urged the colonies to unite against British misrule with the slogan "Join or die" (bottom left). Colonists read the Stamp Act (below).

JOIN or DIE

John Ashe, Cornelius Harnett, Abner Nash, and Hugh Waddell organized the Sons of Liberty in the Wilmington area. On October 19, 1765, about 500 North Carolinians including some Sons of Liberty gathered at Wilmington's courthouse to protest the Stamp Act, which was to take effect thirteen days later on November 1. The crowd hanged a dummy that had been made to look like a British official, then tossed the dummy into their bonfire. They also went from house to house chanting "Liberty, Property, and No Stamp Duty" while collecting more followers.

A dummy of a tax official is hung from a tree limb

The Stamp Act was a total disaster for England. Georgia was the only colony where tax stamps were sold, and not many were sold there. Other colonies besides Massachusetts were now edging closer to violence. On November 16, 1765, about 400 people in Wilmington, North Carolina, marched on the house where North Carolina stamp official Dr. William Houston was staying. Houston was led to the courthouse and advised to quit as North Carolina's stamp distributor. Dr. Houston looked out at the angry mob and did what most of us would do in his shoes. He quit!

Because of all the protests over the Stamp Act, Parliament repealed the law in March 1766. But England kept pushing the Americans to the brink

Colonists dressed as Indians took part in the Boston Tea Party.

of war by passing new tax laws. In 1773 Parliament passed the Tea Act, which lowered the total cost of English tea while still maintaining the tax on it. English lawmakers hoped the Americans would buy the tea because it was a bargain and stop their talk about "taxation without representation." Instead, the Americans threw away quite a bit of English tea!

The best-known such incident took place in Boston on December 16, 1773. That night, fifty patriots dumped 340 chests of English tea into Boston Harbor. To punish Massachusetts for what came to be known as the Boston Tea Party,

Britain closed Boston's port on June 1, 1774. The port closing put many Bostonians out of work and caused a food shortage in the city.

Americans everywhere were starting to feel that "an attack upon the liberties of one Colony is an attack upon the liberties of all," as the Boston patriot Samuel Adams wrote. Several colonies sent food to Boston for its hungry people. North Carolina provided a great deal of food including corn and pork for the Bostonians.

Men in several other colonies held tea parties similar to the famous one in Boston. North Carolina had at least two tea parties that were hosted by women. On October 25, 1774, about fifty women met in Edenton, North Carolina, where they pledged that they would not drink British tea or wear British clothes. This Edenton Tea Party might not sound very bold to us, but in those days when women were kept out of politics it was quite daring. Historians consider the Edenton Tea Party one of the first important political actions by women in any of the colonies during the Revolutionary War era. A few months later, in March 1775, women in Wilmington held a tea party at which they burned British tea.

By the time of the Edenton Tea Party, Americans had begun taking control of their colonial

Samuel Adams

William Hooper

Joseph Hewes

Richard Caswell

governments from the British. Despite Royal Governor Josiah Martin's objections, North Carolina patriots began forming their own government in summer of 1774. Called the North Carolina Provincial Congress, it met in New Bern in late August 1774. The Provincial Congress appointed William Hooper, Joseph Hewes, and Richard Caswell to represent North Carolina at a big meeting that was to be held in Philadelphia, Pennsylvania.

Known as the First Continental Congress, this convention met in Philadelphia from September 5 to October 26, 1774. The First Continental Congress was the seed of a central government for the soon-to-be-born United States, much as the Provincial Congress was the seed of North Carolina's state government. Only Georgia failed to send delegates to the First Continental Congress. The congressmen sent messages to Britain asking that it stop taxing Americans and punishing them for such acts as the Boston Tea Party. They also told all the colonies to get their militias ready in case of war. Before closing, the congressmen made plans to meet again in the spring of 1775 if Britain wouldn't meet their demands.

126

The Battle of Lexington

When the British refused to back down, the stage was set for war. The fighting began at dawn of April 19, 1775, when British troops marched to Lexington, Massachusetts, to arrest Sam Adams and John Hancock. Thanks to Paul Revere's warning, the two leaders escaped, but as they did so British troops and Lexington militia fought a battle on Lexington's village green. The British won the Battle of Lexington, which began the Revolutionary War (1775–1783). Eight Americans were killed and ten were wounded. Only one British soldier was wounded.

John Hancock

The redcoats (as the British troops were nicknamed) went on to nearby Concord, Massachusetts, to seize American war supplies. Word of what had happened at Lexington spread through Massachusetts, drawing hundreds of militiamen to Concord. Just hours after the Battle of Lexington, the Americans defeated the redcoats at Concord's North Bridge, then shot at the Englishmen as they retreated to Boston. By the time the British reached Boston, their losses stood at about 300 dead or wounded. The Americans lost about 100 men in the running Battle of Concord, which was the second battle and America's first victory of the Revolution.

Three weeks after the battles of Lexington and Concord, the Second Continental Congress opened in Philadelphia. Once again William Hooper, Joseph Hewes, and Richard Caswell represented North Carolina. In June 1775, Congress began organizing the Continental Army (forerunner of the U.S. Army) and chose Virginia's George Washington to lead it. During the Revolutionary War all thirteen states (as they were soon calling themselves) provided troops for the Continental Army and also for their own local forces. North Carolina supplied a total of about 20,000 men.

George Washington at the age of forty

While the Second Continental Congress was organizing national affairs, North Carolina was turning itself into a state. In the spring of 1775, the North Carolina Provincial Congress totally replaced the old colonial legislature. Realizing that the North Carolina patriots might seize him, Royal Governor Josiah Martin fled to the British-held Fort Johnston at the mouth of Cape Fear River in May 1775. Martin was the first royal governor forced to flee by the revolutionaries. A short time later, American patriots burned Fort Johnston and former Governor Martin had to take refuge on a British ship in Cape Fear River.

Each of the thirteen colonies had large numbers of Loyalists—people who were loyal to Britain during the Revolutionary War. Although the revolutionaries controlled North Carolina's government, nearly half of all North Carolinians were Loyalists for the first year or so of the war. Ex-Governor Martin hatched a scheme in mid-1775 to take advantage of North Carolina's large Loyalist population. He would raise an army of thousands of North Carolina Loyalists which would be joined by thousands of British soldiers. Together these troops would win back North Carolina for Britain. British officials approved the plan. From his refuge aboard the British ship, Martin sent messages to North Carolina Loyalists that they were to gather around what is now Fayetteville, North Carolina. By early 1776, over 1,500 Loyalists had gathered there.

Under their leader, Donald MacDonald, the Loyalists planned to first seize Wilmington, North Carolina. But Colonel James Moore and his patriot forces in North Carolina had another idea. Moore knew that on their way to Wilmington the Loyalists would cross Moore's Creek Bridge a few miles to the northwest. In February 1776, Moore sent about 1,100 patriot troops under Colonel Richard Caswell and Colonel Alexander Lillington to the bridge. The patriots pulled off many of the bridge planks, then soaped and greased the timbers supporting the planks.

The patriots were hiding in the nearby woods when 1,400 Loyalists reached the bridge on the morning of February 27, 1776. As the Loyalists slipped and slid across the bridge, the Americans opened fire. About 50 Loyalists were killed or wounded in the three minutes of fighting. In addition, about 850 Loyalists were captured and about 2,000 weapons and a large sum of money were seized. Only one patriot was killed and one was wounded at the Battle of Moore's Creek Bridge. The Battle of Moore's Creek Bridge was the first Revolutionary War battle in North Carolina. When the British troops arrived several months later, they decided to give up Martin's plan for conquering North Carolina for the time being.

By this time, Americans were debating a crucial issue. Should the thirteen colonies break free of England and become a new country? Many people felt that even after a long and bloody war, the colonies could return to British rule but with more freedom. However, growing numbers of Americans were deciding that the country was ready for independence.

The Continental Congress in Philadelphia was to vote on the independence issue in early July 1776. Each colony would vote yes or no on whether the country should separate from England. The decision would be made by the majority opinion of the delegates at the Congress. In some cases, the delegates were told how to vote by their home governments. On April 12, 1776, North Carolina's Provincial Congress became the first colonial government to tell its delegates to vote for independence.

The big vote was held on July 2, 1776. North Carolina and every other colony but New York voted for independence that day. New York did not vote on July 2, but made the independence vote unanimous a short time later.

In the days before the independence vote, Thomas Jefferson of Virginia wrote a paper explaining why the thirteen colonies were becoming the United States of America. Congress needed to have this Declaration of Independence ready in case the delegates voted for independence. On July 4, 1776—two days after the big vote—Congress approved the Declaration of Independence. Ever since, Americans have celebrated July 4 as the nation's birthday.

Thomas Jefferson
writing the Declaration
of Independence

Each state's delegates to the Continental Congress signed the Declaration of Independence. William Hooper, Joseph Hewes, and John Penn (who had replaced Richard Caswell in Congress) signed the Declaration for the Tar Heel State. Their signatures can be seen at the top of the second column from the left. Copies of the Declaration went out to all thirteen new states. Across the country, American patriots cheered as the Declaration was read aloud, then rang church bells and shot off 13-gun salutes to celebrate.

John Penn

North Carolina's flag and seal recall the role the state played when America declared its independence. The date "May 20th 1775" can be seen on both the flag and seal. Although we lack written proof, some people think that on this date the people of North Carolina's Mecklenburg County issued a declaration of independence. This "Mecklenburg Declaration of Independence" seems to have been a forerunner to the national Declaration of Independence. The date "April 12th 1776," which appears on the state flag, commemorates the day when North Carolina became the first colony to tell its Continental Congress delegates to vote for independence.

In late 1776 the Provincial Congress drafted

The flag of North Carolina

North Carolina's first state constitution and established its first state government. Also in late 1776, Richard Caswell was chosen North Carolina's first state governor.

To the British, all this talk about independence and state governments was nonsense. They expected to force the United States back into the thirteen colonies. For a while, it appeared that this would happen, because Britain's army and navy were much larger, stronger, and more professional than America's.

Although the British left North Carolina alone for over four years after the Battle of Moore's Creek Bridge, Tar Heels fought in many battles elsewhere. Among them were the battles of Brandywine and Germantown in Pennsylvania (1777), the Battle of Monmouth in New Jersey (1778), and the battles of Charleston and Camden in South Carolina (1780). When Charleston fell to the redcoats in the spring of 1780, nearly 1,500 North Carolinians were among those captured. At the terrible American defeat at the Battle of Camden in August 1780, about half of the 800 Americans killed were Tar Heels.

With the British doing so well in the South, North Carolina's Loyalists began fighting its patriots in mid-1780. This began a two-year period when North Carolina Loyalists and patriots burned each other's farms and killed one another. To make things worse, British General Charles Cornwallis invaded North Carolina with his redcoats in the fall of 1780.

After their loss at Camden, however, the Americans began building their army in the South and plotting better strategy. On October 7, 1780, frontiersmen from Virginia, the Carolinas, Georgia, and Tennessee defeated the British at the Battle of Kings Mountain. It was fought in South Carolina not much more than a gunshot away from the North Carolina border. On January 17, 1781, one thousand Americans, about a third of whom were Tar Heels, beat the British at the Battle of Cowpens, in South Carolina, not far from the North Carolina border.

General Charles Cornwallis

Two months later, a crucial battle took place in North Carolina. Called the Battle of Guilford Courthouse, it was fought near what is now the city of Greensboro on March 15, 1781. On the afternoon of that Tuesday in early spring, about 2,400 redcoats under General Charles Cornwallis attacked 4,500 Americans under General Nathanael Greene at Guilford Courthouse. Although outnumbered 2-1, the British expected to win because their troops were much better

The Battle of Guilford
Courthouse

trained than the North Carolinians and the other Americans. The British claimed victory after this ferocious clash, because the Americans finally retreated from the battlefield. But the redcoats had lost about 650 men compared to about 250 for the Americans. "The Americans fought like demons," Cornwallis reportedly said after this battle. A British politician added, "Another such victory will destroy the British army!"

The Battle of Guilford Courthouse helped bring about the final American triumph. Cornwallis was so weakened by his "victory" at Guilford Courthouse that he abandoned most of North Carolina and withdrew to Yorktown, Virginia, with 8,000 redcoats. There in the fall of 1781, he was surrounded by George Washington's army of 17,000 Americans and Frenchmen. (France had joined America's side in 1778.) Meanwhile, French ships blocked the British from escaping by sea.

Washington inspecting the French batteries at Yorktown

By mid-October, about 600 redcoats had been killed or wounded at Yorktown by the assault from Washington's forces. With no chance to escape or win the battle, Cornwallis surrendered his 7,200 remaining troops to General Washington on October 19, 1781. The American victory at Yorktown was the last major battle of the Revolutionary War. The Americans had won their independence, which even Britain admitted when the peace treaty was signed in 1783.

The surrender of Cornwallis at Yorktown

CORNELIUS HARNETT (1723-1781)

Cornelius Harnett was born on April 20, 1723, probably in the Edenton area of northeastern North Carolina. When he was three years old, Cornelius moved with his family into the Cape Fear River region where Brunswick and Wilmington were being settled. His father was the first sheriff of the county in which these two towns were located.

Cornelius grew up and became a successful merchant. He also entered public service like his father. In 1754, he was elected to represent Wilmington in the North Carolina colonial legislature. He was re-elected to nearly every session of the legislature until the end of colonial times.

The Wilmington area was the most rebellious part of North Carolina when the troubles with Britain began in 1765. As chairman of Wilmington's Sons of Liberty, Harnett was one of the rebel leaders. He so strongly opposed British taxes that people called him "the Samuel Adams of North Carolina." This was a great compliment, because Samuel Adams of Massachusetts was the leading American revolutionary at that time.

Shortly after the Revolutionary War broke out in 1775, Harnett and John Ashe led 300 men to Brunswick, where they burned Fort Johnston. Harnett was also elected to represent Wilmington at the Provincial Congress that turned North Carolina into a state. In the Provincial Congress, he headed the committee that made the famous recommendation for independence on April 12, 1776. He was also on the committee that wrote the first state constitution for North Carolina in late 1776. Then from 1777 to 1780 Harnett represented the Tar Heel State at the Continental Congress in Philadelphia.

The British tried to lure North Carolinians into laying down their arms. They offered to pardon all Tar Heels who stopped fighting—except for two men whom they especially hated. The two exceptions were Cornelius Harnett and Robert Howe, a general who was George Washington's aide.

In early 1780, Cornelius Harnett returned from the Continental Congress to his home in Wilmington. He was sick and exhausted from years of hard work. The British invaded North Carolina a few months after Harnett's return. He tried to escape but the British seized him at a plantation near his home. Since Harnett was too ill to ride a horse or walk, he was tied up by his hands and feet and thrown on a horse "like a sack of meal," according to a witness. Harnett was imprisoned for a short time in Wilmington, which weakened him even more. Harnett died in 1781, shortly after the British let him go—perhaps on the very day of his fifty-eighth birthday. Harnett County in central North Carolina was named for this great patriot.

George Washington presided over the Constitutional Convention.

Chapter VIII

The Twelfth State!

Many [North Carolinians] would have been content to see North Carolina make its own way in the world, remaining totally independent of both Great Britain and all of the other colonies. . . .

From the last paragraph of Colonial North Carolina: A History *by Hugh T. Lefler and William S. Powell*

The signing of the peace treaty with Britain in 1783 did not end America's troubles. In fact, during the 1780s, the country often seemed to be collapsing into thirteen pieces. Each individual state was strong, but the nation as a whole was as weak as a house of cards.

The problem was that the country's central government—still known as the Continental Congress—had little power, and in the early 1780s, most Americans wanted it that way. People were afraid of what a strong government might do. Southerners feared that Northerners might control a strong central government and then boss them around. Small states feared that big states might do the same thing. And just about everyone was terrified that a strong central government would tax them. After fighting a long war with Britain over taxes, the Americans were not going to let their own government do the same thing to them.

At first the nation was governed by the Articles of Confederation. The Articles, which went into effect in spring of 1781, gave the central government little muscle. The country had no national courts, no national money (each state minted its own), no president, and of course no national taxes. The entire U.S. Army had just a few hundred men. The country didn't even have a permanent capital. During the nation's first quarter century, its government moved about between such cities as Philadelphia (Pennsylvania), Baltimore (Maryland), Princeton (New Jersey), and New York City (New York).

The United States paid a terrible price for its weak government. Since there were no taxes, the government had to beg the states for money. Generally, the states gave Congress less than a tenth of the money it needed! The result was that the national government could not pay its bills. Because the U.S. Army was so small, it couldn't put down a revolt by western Massachusetts farmers in 1786–1787, so the Massachusetts militia had to do the job. Because there were no national courts, cases affecting the whole country were difficult to settle. With no president, the country often seemed to be going every which way at once. And since there was no fixed capital, it often happened that most Americans had no idea where their country's government was meeting!

William Blount

By 1787, most people realized that unless the government of the United States was strengthened, the country might be toppled by a rebellion or by a foreign power. To strengthen the central government, American leaders met at Philadelphia, Pennsylvania, between May and September of 1787. Rhode Island was the only state that didn't send delegates to this meeting. North Carolina sent five men.

This convention created a new set of national laws, the U.S. Constitution. Three of North Carolina's delegates signed the Constitution for the Tar Heel State. They were William Blount, who later served as governor of Tennessee; Hugh Williamson, who had been surgeon-general of North Carolina's militia during the Revolution; and Richard D. Spaight, who would serve as North Carolina's governor from 1792 to 1795.

Hugh Williamson

The U.S. Constitution gave the national government more power in many ways. It provided for a

Richard Dobbs Spaight

Supreme Court and other national courts. It
created a powerful Congress that could mint
money, collect taxes, and raise and maintain an
army and navy. It created a strong president. And
it provided for a permanent national capital,
which proved to be Washington, D.C.

The agreement was that each of the thirteen
states would join the country under its Constitution when it approved the document. And when
nine states had approved it, the Constitution
would become the law of the land. Some states
generally liked the Constitution and quickly gave
their approval. Delaware went first on December
7, 1787, and has been called the First State ever
since. Five days later Pennsylvania became the
second state, and six days after that New Jersey
became the third. Several states where many
people opposed the Constitution were slower to
approve it. The Constitution finally took effect
when the ninth state, New Hampshire, approved
it in a tight vote on June 21, 1788.

This left four states—Virginia, New York, North
Carolina, and Rhode Island—in a kind of never-
never land. They were part of the United States,
yet not under its national laws. Virginia left this
never-never land by approving the Constitution
four days after New Hampshire did, and New York

followed suit a month later. In July and August of 1788, North Carolina held a convention in Hillsborough to decide if the state would approve the Constitution. The delegates voted no by a large margin. Thus by late summer of 1788, only North Carolina and Rhode Island held out against the Constitution.

The two had much in common. Because they had welcomed many kinds of people, Rhode Island had been called "Rogue Island" and North Carolina had been dubbed "Rogues' Haven" in colonial days. The people of both colonies were very protective of their rights and not afraid to defy the rest of the nation. And both states saw a big flaw in the Constitution. There was no Bill of Rights to guarantee certain basic rights to Americans.

The process of adding a Bill of Rights to the U.S. Constitution was underway by the fall of 1789. This was one reason why a North Carolina convention in Fayetteville approved the Constitution on November 21, 1789, by a 195-77 vote. With that vote, North Carolina became our twelfth state. That same year, North Carolina gave up its claim to the region that became the state of Tennessee. On May 29, 1790, Rhode Island finally became the last of the original thirteen colonies to approve the Constitution.

During the Revolutionary War and for a few years afterward, North Carolina's capital was moved from place to place. In 1792, the North Carolina legislature chose a site for a permanent state capital not far from the middle of the state. The new town that was laid out there became the state's permanent capital in 1794, and has been so ever since. This town was named Raleigh for Sir Walter Raleigh, the man who began colonizing North Carolina more than 400 years ago.

The capitol building at Raleigh in the 1850s

JAMES IREDELL (1751-1799)

The oldest of five children, James Iredell was born in England. When James was 15, his father suffered a stroke that forced him to retire as a merchant. James had to work to help support his family. Through the influence of wealthy relatives, James was made comptroller of customs at Edenton, North Carolina, when he was only 17. It was his job to keep track of the taxes that ships had to pay when they sailed into Edenton.

James reached Edenton around New Year's Day of 1769. He served as a customs official for seven years. In the journal he began when he was 18, James criticized himself for "spending too much time in an idle, unprofitable manner." The record shows just the opposite, however. Besides working as a customs official, he studied law and began a second career as a lawyer around the age of 20. In addition, he helped his wealthy uncle in British-ruled Jamaica conduct business in America. Jemmy, as he was called, also found time to fall in love with Hannah Johnston, his law teacher's sister. James wrote poems about Hannah and gazed out of his office windows in hopes of seeing her walking through Edenton. Hannah felt the same way about James and in 1773, they were married.

Meanwhile, the troubles with England had begun. Although he had been in America only a few years and was a government official, James sided with his new country. He was happy to be involved in "the noblest of all causes, a struggle for Freedom," as he wrote to a friend. His rich uncle in Jamaica planned to leave James his fortune until he learned that James took the American side. The uncle then threatened to leave his fortune to someone else unless the young man gave up his rebellious ways. This didn't stop James from writing about British injustice and doing all he could to help America win its freedom. James never got the inheritance, but he became one of America's most important leaders.

James Iredell worked as North Carolina's attorney general (head law officer) and also as a judge during the war. After the war, he organized all of North Carolina's laws. Iredell was also one of the people most responsible for convincing North Carolina leaders to approve the U.S. Constitution on November 21, 1789.

The Supreme Court was one of the governmental bodies created by the U.S. Constitution. President George Washington admired Iredell's legal ability and in 1790 appointed him to the highest court in the land. At 38, Iredell was the youngest member of the Supreme Court at the time. He was an outstanding justice and was involved in some decisions of lasting importance. However, the job involved a great deal of travel, which ruined his health. This man who had done so much so early in life died in Edenton when he was only 48 years old. North Carolina's Iredell County was named for him.

RICHARD DOBBS SPAIGHT (1758–1802)

Richard Dobbs Spaight was born in New Bern into a well-known political family. His father held several major posts in North Carolina. His uncle on his mother's side, Arthur Dobbs, was North Carolina's governor between 1754 and 1765.

When Richard was still a child, his world came crashing down. His uncle, the governor, died in 1765. Soon after that, both of Richard's parents died. The boy was sent to his father's birthplace, Ireland. He went to school in Ireland and then attended the University of Glasgow in Scotland before returning to North Carolina in 1778.

The America to which Richard returned was fighting for its life in the Revolutionary War. He served for a time in the American army, and in 1779, at just 21 years of age, he was elected to the North Carolina legislature. Between 1783 and 1785, Spaight represented the Tar Heel State in the Continental Congress. Then in 1787, he was one of its delegates to the Constitutional Convention.

Spaight made a common-sense suggestion soon after the Convention opened. He said that even after the delegates passed an article of the Constitution, they should be free to change their minds. That way no decision was final until the Constitution was finished. His idea was approved. After returning to North Carolina, he worked to have his state approve the Constitution.

In 1792, Spaight was elected governor of North Carolina. He was governor when the state government moved to Raleigh in 1794, and in early 1795 he opened the University of North Carolina at Chapel Hill.

During his last years, Spaight served in the U.S. House of Representatives and in the North Carolina state senate. By 1802, he was involved in a bitter feud with North Carolina lawmaker John Stanly. Although details are missing, we know that the two men were leaders of rival political parties, and that Stanly insulted Spaight by saying that he had faked illness to avoid certain votes in Congress. Today lawmakers often argue by calling each other names on TV and in newspapers. But until the mid-1800s, Americans sometimes fought gun duels to settle quarrels, which was what Spaight and Stanly decided to do.

The duel was fought on September 5, 1802, behind a building on the outskirts of New Bern. It was said that by this time Spaight was so sick he could barely hold his pistol. As a crowd watched, the two men stood back to back ten steps apart. At a signal, they both turned and fired. Their first shots missed, but Stanly's fourth shot struck Spaight. The former governor of North Carolina died the next day, leaving a wife and three young children. One of them, six-year-old Richard Dobbs Spaight, Jr., grew up to be the governor of the Tar Heel State in 1835–1836.

Richard Dobbs Spaight

First page of the Carolina Charter, 1663

The modell drawen vp by the Lo: Ashley ffor the gou't
of Carolina

With this designe the Lo: proprieators who are at great charge for
carrying on ye plantac̄on haue put ye frameing of a gou't in the
hands of one whose pts & dependents in affaires of State are
vniuersally agreed on, and who is by all men allowed to knowe
It is expedient foundac̄ons as may be equall safe & lasting
and to this hath a full large onic̄on to wish well to mankind
and to desire y't all the people yt he hath to doe might be happy.
The Lo: Ashley ffor by the consent of his brethern the rest of the
proprieators hath drawen vpto ye generall satisfac̄on found
fundamentall constitutions w'ch are since by ye joynt approbac̄o
confirmed to be the modell & forme of gou't in the prouince of
Carolina The main designe and ballance yrof according to the best
of my memorie hauing had a coppy yrof in short is as followes

1 Every Countie is to consist of 40 square plotts each conteining 12000
acres; of these square plots each of the proprieators is to haue one
w'ch is to be called a seigniory eight more of those square plots
are to be dibyddit amongst the three noblemen of yt Countie
A landgraue who is to haue foure of yu, and two Cassiques
who are to haue two apiece And these square plots belonging to the
Nobility are to be called Barronies The oyr 24 square plots
called Collonies are to be the porc̄on of ye people & this method is
to be obserued in the planting & setting out of the whole Countrie
So yt one fifth of ye land is to be in the proprieators and fifth
in the nobility and three fifths in the people

2 The seigniories & barronies yt is the hereditarie lands belonging to
the proprieators and nobility are all intirely to descend to ye aires w't ye
dignity w'thout power of alienac̄on more yn for their lives or
21 yeares or two thirds of ye seigniories & barronies and the rest
to be the damasene

3 There will be also some mannors in the Collonies but none lesse yn
3000 acres in apiece w'ch like the rest of the Collonie lands
will be alienable only w't this difference yt it be not parcelled out
but if sold it must be altogether

4 There is to be a Biennall p'liam't consisting of eight proprieators the
landgraues and cassiques and one out of every precinct that is
the sixt neighbouring Collonies for the people chosen by the
freeholders These are to sitt and vote altogether for the making
of Lawes w'ch shall be in force no longer then 60 yeares after
their enacting The greatest mischief of most gou'm'ts by w'ch not
only the people are mightily intangled by multiplicity of rules and
penalties

The Fundamental Constitutions of Carolinas written in 1669

In CONGRESS, July 4, 1776

The unanimous Declaration of the thirteen united States of America.

The Declaration of Independence

Colonial America Time Line

Before the arrival of Europeans, many millions of Indians belonging to dozens of tribes lived in North America (and also in Central and South America)

About 982 A.D.—Eric the Red, born in Norway, reaches Greenland during one of the first European voyages to North America

About 985—Eric the Red brings settlers from Iceland to Greenland

About 1000—Leif Ericson (Eric the Red's son) leads what is thought to be the first European expedition to mainland North America; Leif probably lands in Canada

1492—Christopher Columbus, sailing for Spain, reaches America

1497—John Cabot reaches Canada in the first English voyage to North America

1513—Ponce de León of Spain explores Florida

1519-1521—Hernando Cortés of Spain conquers Mexico

1565—St. Augustine, Florida, the first permanent European town in what is now the United States, is founded by the Spanish

1607—Jamestown, Virginia, is founded, the first permanent English town in the present-day United States

1608—Frenchman Samuel de Champlain founds the village of Quebec, Canada

1609—Henry Hudson explores the eastern coast of present-day United States for The Netherlands; the Dutch then claim parts of New York, New Jersey, Delaware, and Connecticut and name the area New Netherland

1619—Virginia's House of Burgesses, America's first representative lawmaking body, is founded

1619—The first shipment of black slaves arrives in Jamestown

1620—English Pilgrims found Massachusetts' first permanent town at Plymouth

1621—Massachusetts Pilgrims and Indians hold the famous first Thanksgiving feast in colonial America

1622—Indians kill 347 settlers in Virginia

1623—Colonization of New Hampshire is begun by the English

1624—Colonization of present-day New York State is begun by the Dutch at Fort Orange (Albany)

1625—The Dutch start building New Amsterdam (now New York City)

1630—The town of Boston, Massachusetts, is founded by the English Puritans

1633—Colonization of Connecticut is begun by the English

1634—Colonization of Maryland is begun by the English

1635—Boston Latin School, the colonies' first public school, is founded

1636—Harvard, the colonies' first college, is founded in Massachusetts

1636—Rhode Island colonization begins when Englishman Roger Williams founds Providence

1638—The colonies' first library is established at Harvard

1638—Delaware colonization begins when Swedish people build Fort Christina at present-day Wilmington

1640—Stephen Daye of Cambridge, Massachusetts, prints *The Bay Psalm Book*, the first English-language book published in what is now the United States

1643—Swedish settlers begin colonizing Pennsylvania

1647—Massachusetts forms the first public school system in the colonies

1650—North Carolina is colonized by Virginia settlers in about this year

1650—Population of colonial United States is about 50,000

1660—New Jersey colonization is begun by the Dutch at present-day Jersey City

1670—South Carolina colonization is begun by the English near Charleston

1673—Jacques Marquette and Louis Jolliet explore the upper Mississippi River for France

1675-76—New England colonists beat Indians in King Philip's War

1682—Philadelphia, Pennsylvania, is settled

1682—La Salle explores Mississippi River all the way to its mouth in Louisiana and claims the whole Mississippi Valley for France

1693—College of William and Mary is founded in Williamsburg, Virginia

1700—Colonial population is about 250,000

1704—*The Boston News-Letter*, the first successful newspaper in the colonies, is founded

1706—Benjamin Franklin is born in Boston

1732—George Washington, future first president of the United States, is born in Virginia

1733—English begin colonizing Georgia, their thirteenth colony in what is now the United States

1735—John Adams, future second president, is born in Massachusetts

1743—Thomas Jefferson, future third president, is born in Virginia

1750—Colonial population is about 1,200,000

1754—France and England begin fighting the French and Indian War over North American lands

1763—England, victorious in the war, gains Canada and most other French lands east of the Mississippi River

1764—British pass Sugar Act to gain tax money from the colonists

1765—British pass the Stamp Act, which the colonists despise; colonists then hold the Stamp Act Congress in New York City

1766—British repeal the Stamp Act

1770—British soldiers kill five Americans in the "Boston Massacre"

1773—Colonists dump British tea into Boston Harbor at the "Boston Tea Party"

1774—British close up port of Boston to punish the city for the tea party

1774—Delegates from all the colonies but Georgia meet in Philadelphia at the First Continental Congress

1775—**April 19:** Revolutionary War begins at Lexington and Concord, Massachusetts

      May 10: Second Continental Congress convenes in Philadelphia

      June 17: Colonists inflict heavy losses on British but lose Battle of Bunker Hill near Boston

      July 3: George Washington takes command of Continental Army

1776—**March 17:** Washington's troops force the British out of Boston in the first major American victory of the war

      May 4: Rhode Island is first colony to declare itself independent of Britain

July 4: Declaration of Independence is adopted

December 26: Washington's forces win Battle of Trenton (New Jersey)

1777—January 3: Americans win at Princeton, New Jersey

August 16: Americans win Battle of Bennington at New York-Vermont border

September 11: British win Battle of Brandywine Creek near Philadelphia

September 26: British capture Philadelphia

October 4: British win Battle of Germantown near Philadelphia

October 17: About 5,000 British troops surrender at Battle of Saratoga in New York

December 19: American army goes into winter quarters at Valley Forge, Pennsylvania, where more than 3,000 soldiers die by spring

1778—February 6: France joins the American side

July 4: American George Rogers Clark captures Kaskaskia, Illinois, from the British

1779—February 23-25: George Rogers Clark captures Vincennes in Indiana

September 23: American John Paul Jones captures British ship *Serapis*

1780—May 12: British take Charleston, South Carolina

August 16: British badly defeat Americans at Camden, South Carolina

October 7: Americans defeat British at Kings Mountain, South Carolina

1781—January 17: Americans win battle at Cowpens, South Carolina

March 1: Articles of Confederation go into effect as laws of the United States

March 15: British suffer heavy losses at Battle of Guilford Courthouse in North Carolina; British then give up most of North Carolina

October 19: British army under Charles Cornwallis surrenders at Yorktown, Virginia, as major Revolutionary War fighting ends

1783—September 3: United States officially wins Revolution as the United States and Great Britain sign Treaty of Paris

November 25: Last British troops leave New York City

1787—On December 7, Delaware becomes the first state by approving the U.S. Constitution

1788—On June 21, New Hampshire becomes the ninth state when it approves the U.S. Constitution; with nine states having approved it, the Constitution goes into effect as the law of the United States

1789—On April 30, George Washington is inaugurated as first president of the United States

1790—On May 29, Rhode Island becomes the last of the original thirteen colonies to become a state

1791—U.S. Bill of Rights goes into effect on December 15

INDEX- *Page numbers in boldface type indicate illustrations.*

About the Author

Dennis Brindell Fradin is the author of more than 100 published children's books. His works for Childrens Press include the Young People's Stories of Our States series, the Disaster! series, and the Thirteen Colonies series. His other books are *Remarkable Children* (Little, Brown), which is about twenty children who made history, and a science-fiction novel entitled *How I Saved the World* (Dillon). Dennis is married to Judith Bloom Fradin, a high-school English teacher. They have two sons named Tony and Mike and a daughter named Diana Judith. Dennis was graduated from Northwestern University in 1967 with a B.A. in creative writing, and has lived in Evanston, Illinois, since that year.

Photo Credits